UNIVERSITY OF CALGARY

Purchasing Power Parity, balanced Growth, and Volatility Forecasting:

An Application of Recent Developments in Time Series Analysis

by

Periklis Gogas

A THESIS

SUBMITTED TO THE FACULTY OF GRADUATE STUDIES

IN PARTIAL FULFILLMENT OF THE REQUIREMENTS FOR THE

DEGREE OF DOCTOR OF PHILOSOPHY

DEPARTMENT OF ECONOMICS

CALGARY, ALBERTA

JUNE, 2000

National Library
of Canada

Bibliothèque nationale
du Canada

Acquisitions and
Bibliographic Services

Acquisitions et
services bibliographiques

395 Wellington Street
Ottawa ON K1A 0N4
Canada

395, rue Wellington
Ottawa ON K1A 0N4
Canada

Your file Votre référence

Our file Notre référence

The author has granted a non-exclusive licence allowing the National Library of Canada to reproduce, loan, distribute or sell copies of this thesis in microform, paper or electronic formats.

The author retains ownership of the copyright in this thesis. Neither the thesis nor substantial extracts from it may be printed or otherwise reproduced without the author's permission.

L'auteur a accordé une licence non exclusive permettant à la Bibliothèque nationale du Canada de reproduire, prêter, distribuer ou vendre des copies de cette thèse sous la forme de microfiche/film, de reproduction sur papier ou sur format électronique.

L'auteur conserve la propriété du droit d'auteur qui protège cette thèse. Ni la thèse ni des extraits substantiels de celle-ci ne doivent être imprimés ou autrement reproduits sans son autorisation.

0-612-54780-9

Canadä

ABSTRACT

In this thesis, I use recent advance in statistics and econometrics in an effort to re-test some well-known theoretical propositions, examine whether those new techniques support the theory, provide models that are better fitted to describe and forecast economic time-series. The Purchasing Power Parity theory is tested using the Fisher and Seater (1993) and King and Watson (1997) methodologies and strong evidence in support of PPP is found. I use the general class of ARCH/GARCH processes to model financial time series in an ARIMA framework and the best fitted models outperform traditional ARIMA models in terms of the forecast variance. Finally, I test the balanced growth theory and try to estimate a money demand function using the Johansen and Juselius (1993) methodology. I do not find evidence in support of the balanced growth theory and a stable money demand function, and these results are not sensitive to different monetary aggregates that are constructed according to recent index number theory.

ACKNOWLEDGEMENTS

I would like to thank, and not only because it is customary to do so, my supervisor Dr. Apostolos Serletis, for all the invaluable help that both in academics and elsewhere that he plentifully offered me during my studies at the University of Calgary. I truly appreciate his constant guidance, support and motivation throughout the research for this thesis, and also his family, Aglaia, Demitre, and Anna, who were my family away from home all these years.

I thank also, my Ph.D. committee, Dr. Daniel Gordon and Dr. Christopher Bruce from the Department of Economics, Dr. Sick from the Faculty of Management, Dr. Tak Fung from Information Technologies and Dr. Douglas Fisher from the Department of Economics at North Carolina State University.

The only person who can actually understand what I went through these years for this degree, is of course my friend and fellow PbD. student, David P. Krause. David, "That's good stuff'.

The financial support by the Department of Economics in the form of Teaching and Research Assistantships is greatly appreciated.

Last, but not least, I thank my parents, George and Evagelia, and my brothers, Thanasis and Dimitris, that supported me throughout my endeavors in Canada.

Στους γονείς μου
Γιώργο και Ευαγγελία

Στα αδέρφια μου
Θανάση και Δημήτρη

Και σ' εκείνη...

TABLE OF CONTENTS

LIST OF TABLES

CHAPTER 1

INTRODUCTION

During the last decade we have seen major innovations that affected with one or another way all areas of statistics, econometrics and applied economics. Following the 1970's and 1980's that can be referred to as the decades of theory development, the 1990's were highlighted by major developments in statistics and econometrics. Thus, we observe the development and implementation of new techniques that resolve many of the problems md impediments in the use of classical econometric procedures. In time series analysis, whenever researchers used the classical econometric models to describe the relationship between certain economic variables, to test different hypotheses or to forecast future values of these variables, implicitly assumed that the assumptions these models make, regarding specific properties of the data in hand, were met. Some of the basic assumptions are that the first moments of the series in question must be stationary or in other words that the mean and variance of the series must be constant. Testing economic times series for these properties, has led us to the conclusion that most series do not satisfy either one or both of these assumptions. Therefore, the empirical results that are based on these techniques are invalid. The solution to this problem is the use of econometric methods specifically designed for series that fail to satisfy the assumptions of the classical econometric models or the transformation of the time series data in such a manner that they conform to the assumptions.

From the techniques that were developed in the past decade to deal with non-stationary and heteroscedastic data, I will employ in this thesis some of the most recent developments and apply them in some areas of economic theory, in an effort to see whether the implementation of these procedures provides evidence in support of the previous literature. I wilt show in this thesis that the use of these methodologies lead to some very interesting propositions and theory implications that were not obvious in the previous literature.

In all three empirical cases, Chapters 2, 3, and 4, the stationarity properties of the economic time series are of great importance for the techniques that are used. The issue of homoscedasticity in the context of an ARIMA framework is raised in Chapter 3. The traditional Box-Jenkings methodology where a constant variance is assumed, is proven inadequate especially for forecasts and it is replaced by explicitly modeling the conditional variance of the time series. In Chapter 4, I test the balanced growth theory of development economics and at the same time try to test for the existence of a stable money demand function. In doing so, I use both the simple sum monetary aggregates that are very common in the literature, and also the Divisia and currency equivalent monetary indices that are not common at all but they are more appropriate, from a theoretical point of view, as the recent literature suggests. Using these different measures of monetary aggregates we can see how sensitive the results are to the different methods of aggregation.

Chapter 2 of this thesis, deals with the theory of Purchasing Power Parity (PPP). Purchasing power parity and the law of one price is a core assumption in the field of international economics.

Three different approaches have been used in the literature to test for PPP. The first approach, following Engle and Granger (1987), is to test whether the relative price ratio and the exchange rate are cointegrated. If they are, then this is viewed as evidence in support of PPP. Another similar approach is to use the Johansen (1988) multivariate maximum likelihood generalization of the Engle and Granger (1987) methodology. Again, in this case whenever the domestic and foreign price levels and the exchange rates are found to be cointegrated and the cointegrating vector satisfies certain conditions, this is evidence in favor of PPP. Finally, the third approach is to test the real exchange rate for stationarity. If the real exchange rate is mean reverting then PPP holds, but if the hypothesis of a stochastic trend cannot be rejected, then PPP does not hold.

Thus, the common theme, according to these studies, is that when the relative price level and the exchange rate are not level-stationary, cointegration is a necessary condition for PPP to hold. In Chapter 2 of this thesis, I test for PPP employing more recent techniques in time series analysis. Namely, I use the Fisher and Seater (1993) and the King and Watson (1997) methodologies. These methodologies allow the testing of long-run neutrality propositions taking advantage of recent advances in the theory of nonstationary regressors. According to these methodologies tests for such long-run run propositions can be constructed only if the variables in question satisfy certain nonstationarity conditions. Most of the previous literature ignored these requirements.

Fisher and Seater (1993) used their methodology to test for long-run neutrality and superneutrality of money, and King and Watson (1997) tested not only for long-run neutrality and superneutrality of money but also the Fisher effect, and the long-run Phillips curve. More recently, Serletis and Koustas (1998) use the King and Watson (1997) methodology and long, low-frequency data to test the neutrality and superneutrality of money propositions in ten OECD countries and Koustas and Serletis (1999) use the same methodology to test the Fisher effect.

4

Testing long-run classical neutrality propositions, using the Fisher and Seater (1993) and King and Watson (1997) methodologies, requires that the series are nonstationary and do not cointegrate.

Thus, although in the previous literature whenever the relative price ratio and the exchange rate were found to be non-stationary but not cointegrated, researchers concluded that PPP does not hold. However, using the Fisher and Seater (1993) and King and Watson (1997) methodologies, we may still find the long-run derivative or the long-run multiplier respectively, to be equal to one and therefore conclude that PPP holds in the long-run. That is, the absence of cointegration, that for the previous literature implied that PPP does not hold, in this case simply directs us to different testing procedures. In particular to the use of the Fisher and Seater (2993) and the King and Watson (1997) methodologies, according to which cointegration is not a sufficient nor a necessary condition for PPP to hold.

In Chapter 3, I use the Box-Jenkings methodology to model the historical evolution, and produce in-sample forecasts for six energy future prices, crude oil, electricity, heating oil, natural gas, propane and unleaded gas, taking into consideration the conditional variance of the disturbances. In contrast to the unconditional variance, which refers to the variance of the population, or the variance of the sample, the conditional variance is a function of past realizations of shocks that are known in the present period. These past shocks tend to affect the volatility of the series in subsequent periods, and modeling the conditional variance allows one to produce better estimates of future volatility. Especially in financial time series data, it is more important to be able to forecast the conditional variance of an asset's returns than using the unconditional variance. The later describes the volatility of the asset over its life-span, information that may not be very useful to an investor if her holding period is relatively small. A forecast of the variance of the asset a few periods ahead, given past history, will be more appropriate.

The series that I use in Chapter 3, are found to be nonstationary and thus I apply the best fitted ARIMA representation. In doing so, I find that one of the assumptions of classical estimation and hypothesis testing procedures is violated in all six data series. That is, the variance of the error term is not stationary over time, as it is required, but we can observe volatility clustering' periods where the volatility of these future variables is high and other periods where it is low. Thus, the assumption of homoscedasticity does not hold. Formally testing, according to Engle (1982), I find evidence of ARC/GARCH processes in the data, which means that the conditional variance of the disturbances can be modeled and estimated, and use it to achieve a better fit and produce more accurate forecasts.

The literature shows that, in general, models that take into account the conditional heteroscedasticity tend to perform better than other models (homoscedastic, autoregressive, or non-parametric), in short forecast horizons.

In the effort to model the conditional heteroscedasticity, several specifications of the conditional variance are tested, with different lag structures for each one. I compare the goodness of fit of the ARCH, GARCH, ARCH-M, and EGARCH models, proposed by Engle (1982), Bollerslev (1986), Engle, Lilien and Robins (1987) and Nelson (1991) respectively. I select the best model using likelihood ratio tests and the Akaike and Swartz information critiria

Finally the best fitted models are used for in-sample forecasts and the conditional variance provides the 95% confidence band for these estimates. The five-day ahead forecasts of the unconditional and the conditional standard deviations axe then used for comparisons.

In Chapter 4, I use a real business cycle model, to test for the balanced growth theory and at the same time for the existence of a stable money demand function. According to this theory, at the steady state of the economy, per capita output, consumption and investment grow at the same rate over time and thus, the great ratios, consumption - output and investment - output must be constant. This means that these three time series variables must satisfy certain restrictions in the steady state in order for the balanced growth theory to hold. In particular, they must not be stationary, and the order of integration of the three variables must be the same and they should also cointegrate so that the great ratios remain stationary.

In the system that is estimated in this Chapter, the presence of a stable money demand function is examined as well. As I discussed above, for the balanced growth theory to hold, output must have a unit root. In order for a stable money demand function to exist this also means that money, interest rates, and output must be integrated of the same order and cointegrated. But what money measure should we use to test for the money demand function? The developments-in recent years in statistics and econometrics are not only constrained on how time series data are used in econometric models, but also these developments show how these data series must be constructed in order to actually reflect and measure properly a specific variable.

Thus, the important breakthroughs in index number theory, show that some economic data are not constructed properly and these problems in measurement may have implications in tests of economic theory. One important variable that leading researchers in index number theory have argued that is not measured correctly is money. The derivation of different money measures, from the narrowest definitions to the most broad ones, using simple sum techniques was proven to be wrong by the recent literature. Thus, in order to avoid the critique that firstly William Barnett voiced and later more researchers sided with, I use three different monetary aggregation procedures to distinguish between simple-sum, Divisia and currency equivalent monetary aggregates. Four different levels of aggregation for each of the three monetary aggregation procedures are used, for a total of twelve different time series for the money variable. In this fashion, I will be able to test the sensitivity of the results to different definitions of money. Whenever, a cointegrating relationship is found that is in accordance with the theory, variable shocks to the system are applied, to test the dynamics and the stability of the identified relations.

In Chapter 5, I present the conclusions that are drawn from this thesis.

CHAPTER 2

NEW INTERNATIONAL EVIDENCE ON THE THEORY OF

PURCHASING POWER PARITY

2.1 INTRODUCTION

The theory of Purchasing Power Parity (PPP) is the core assumption in the exchange rate models in international economics. In the case of fixed exchange rates it explains why the domestic inflation rate must be equal to the foreign inflation rate, and under a floating exchange rates regime provides a theory of exchange rate determination. In the later case which is the most interesting today, PPP provides a benchmark for policy makers and exchange traders.

The theory of purchasing power parity has been studied extensively recently using new advances in econometrics. In general these studies, and especially the ones that concern the floating exchange rates period, find little evidence in support of PPP. See for example, Adler and Lehman (1983), Patel (1990), Grilli and Kaminski (1991), Flynn and Boucher (1993), Serletis (1994), Serletis and Zimonopoulos (1997), and Dueker and Serletis (1997). Other studies, such as Frenkel (1980), Diebold, Husted and Rush (1991), Glen (1992), Peron and Vogelsang (1992), Phylaktis and Kassimatis (1994), and Lothian and Taylor (1996), using different groups of countries or longer periods of time or pairs of countries with big differences in their inflation rates, report evidence in support of PPP.

In testing the theory of PPP, some studies have applied Engle and Granger (1987) bivariate cointegration tests to the exchange rates and the relative price levels, as for example, Pippenger (1993). Other studies have used Johansen's (1988) maximum likelihood extension to Engle and Granger's methodology to test PPP in a multivariate framework - e.g. Johansen and Juselius (1992), Kugler and Lenz (1993) and Serletis (1994).

Another test for PPP is to test whether the real exchange rate has a unit root. If it does, then PPP is rejected - see for example, Phylaktis and Kassimatis (1994), Dueker and Serletis (1997), and Serletis and Zimonopoulos (1997). Serletis and Zimonopoulos (1997), examine the U.S. dollar and DM-based real exchange rates for 17 OECD countries and find that the unit root hypothesis for the real exchange rate cannot be rejected even when they allow for a possible change in the level, according to Perron and Vogelsang (1992). This result persists even when they test the dollar-based real exchange rate using the more general fractional integration tests.

In this paper I will test PPP using two recent approaches for testing long-run propositions that use recent advances in the theory of nonstationary regressors. These approaches show that meaningful tests can only be constructed if the variables satisfy certain nonstationarity conditions. Most of the existing literature ignores these issues and thus those tests are invalid. I will adopt the Fisher and Seater (1993) methodology in the context of PPP. Fisher and Seater (1993) used the long-run multiplier to test for long-run neutrality and superneutrality of money in an ARIMA framework. Also, I will use the King and Watson (1997) nonstructural bivariate autoregressive methodology. King and Watson test the neutrality and superneutrality of money, the Fisher Effect and the long-run Phillips curve - see Serletis and Koustas (1998), and Koustas and Serletis (1998) for some applications.

In section 2, I briefly discuss the theory of PPP, in section 3 I investigate the integration and cointegration properties of the variables since this is crucial for testing PPP.

In sections 4 and 5 I test PPP using the Fisher and Seater (1993) and King and Watson (1997) approaches, respectively. Finally in section 6 I summarize the conclusions.

2.2 THEORETICAL FOUNDATIONS OF PPP

Purchasing Power Parity is one of the best known relationships in international economics. According to PPP, the relationship between the exchange rate and the domestic and foreign price levels is given by:

$$S_t = A\frac{P_t}{P_t^*}, \quad (2.2.1)$$

where S_t represents the exchange rate in terms of domestic currency per unit of the foreign currency, P_t is the domestic price level, P_t^* is the foreign price level and A is an arbitrary constant. Thus, the data series that are needed to test PPP are the exchange rate S_t, and the price ratio P_t / P_t^*. Taking the logarithms the above relation becomes:

$$s_t = a + p_t - p_t^*, \quad (2.2.2)$$

where lower-case letters denote the logarithms of A, S_t, P_t, and P_t^*.

The assumptions underlying PPP is that the price indices in the two countries include the same goods with the same weights, and the goods are freely tradable in the two countries. Freely means that there are no impediments to international trade such as tariffs and quotas. Under these assumptions, if PPP does not hold, it would be possible to profit from arbitrage between the two countries. Although in the definition of PPP we assume that all goods that are included in the price indices are freely traded, there are some kinds of goods such as services that are non-traded. Another issue with respect to PPP is that it is unlikely that it will hold continuously at every point in time. As Cassel, who is recognized as the formulator of the PPP relationship, notes, a number of factors such as the international capital mobility in terms of speculation against certain currencies, and government interventions can cause the spot exchange rate to deviate from the PPP benchmark in the sort-run. For these reasons, we recognize that PPP is more likely to hold in the long-run.

In the effort to test PPP, many researchers have applied Engle and Granger (1987) bivariate cointegration tests to the spot exchange rate and the relative price level series. In these studies, when the two series are found to be cointegrated, this is viewed as evidence that PPP holds. In the opposite case, where the exchange rate and the price ratio series, do not cointegrate the researchers conclude that PPP does not hold.

Following the Fisher and Seater (1993) reasoning on money neutrality applied to PPP, I point out that evidence that the exchange rate and the relative price series do cointegrate, is neither necessary or sufficient to accept PPP. Cointegration means that even if the two series are non-stationary, there is a linear combination of the two variables that is stationary. Cointegration alone does not tell us anything about PPP. We can reject PPP

13

in presence of cointegration if one of the following is true: the coefficient of the relative price when it is the independent variable in the cointegrating equation is statistically different than one, or when the source of the non-stationarity is not the relative price variable but the exchange rate. A Granger-causality test may be suitable to test this.

On the other hand, rejection of cointegration does not mean that PPP does not hold. Cointegration is a linear relationship between two variables and PPP pertains to the long-run relationship of these variables. So it is possible that although the exchange rate and the relative price do not cointegrate, there is a long-run effect of the relative price to the exchange rate. The Fisher and Seater (1993) and King and Watson (1997) tests that I employ in this paper, provide estimates of the long-run derivative of the relative price to the exchange rate when the two series are not cointegrated. If this long-run derivative is not statistically different than one then I conclude that PPP holds.

From this discussion it becomes obvious that cointegration tests have nothing to say with respect to PPP per se and other long-run relationships. They only provide direction to what is the appropriate method to use in testing these relationships.

Since for both the Fisher and Seater (1993) and the King and Watson (1997) procedures the integration and cointegration properties of the data, as we have seen, are of critical importance, I need first to investigate these properties of the data.

2.3 INTEGRATION AND COINTEGRATION TESTS

For both the Fisher and Seater (1993) and the King and Watson (1997) tests that I am going to use to test PPP, the integration and cointegration properties of the data are of

14

great importance as it will be explained in the next two sections in the discussion of these testing procedures. The data that I use are the consumer price index ratios and the U.S. dollar-based exchange rates for 16 OECD countries. The CPI ratios are constructed as:

$$P_t = \frac{CPI_t}{CPI_{US,t}}, \qquad (2.3.1)$$

where CPI is the consumer price index in the respective country, and CPI_{US} is the consumer price index for the United States. The data are quarterly, ranging from the first quarter of 1973 to the second quarter of 1997, and they are from the I.M.F. International Financial Statistics publications. Data before 1973 would not be appropriate for this analysis because of the fixed exchange rate system that was in effect in that period.

2.3.1   UNIT ROOT TESTS

In testing for stochastic trends (unit roots) in the autoregressive representation of each individual time series, I use two alternative unit root testing procedures to deal with the fact that some times the data are not very informative about whether or not there is a unit root. In the first and second column of panel A of Tables 2.1 and 2.2 I report the test statistics for the augmented Dickey-Fuller (ADF) test[1] and the nonparametric (PP) test of Phillips and Perron (1988). The tests statistics are calculated using SHAZAM 7.0. I use the

---

[1] See Dickey and Fuller (1981).

PP test since it is robust to a wide variety of serial correlation and time-dependent heteroscedasticity. For both the ADF and the PP tests the optimal lag length is taken to be as the highest significant lag order at the 95% significance level from either the autocorrelation function or the partial autocorrelation function of the first differenced series up to a maximum of $\sqrt{N}$, where N is the number of observations. The regression equation for the augmented Dickey-Fuller test is:

$$\Delta Y_t = \alpha_0 + \alpha_1 t + \alpha_2 Y_{t-1} + \sum_{i=1}^{p} \beta_i \Delta Y_{t-i} + \varepsilon_t. \quad (2.3.2)$$

As an alternative to using the lags to correct for serial correlation, the Phillips-Perron method uses non-parametric correction. I first estimate equation (2.3.2) with p=0 and then the statistics are transformed to remove the effects of serial correlation on their asymptotic distribution. For the formula of the transformation of the statistics see Perron (1988, Table 1, p.308-9). The critical values are the same as in the Dickey-Fuller tests. The Newey and West (1987) method is used to estimate the error variance from the estimated residuals as:

$$\frac{1}{N}\sum_{t=1}^{N} \varepsilon_t^2 + \frac{2}{N}\sum_{s=1}^{p} \omega(s,p) \sum_{t=s+1}^{N} \varepsilon_t \varepsilon_{t-s} \quad (2.3.3)$$

where p is a truncation lag parameter and $\omega(s,p) = \dfrac{1-s}{p+1}$.

The critical value for the tests with a constant and time trend at a 95% significance level is 6.25. Based on this critical value and the test statistics reported in panel A of Table 2.1, the null hypothesis of a unit root in the log levels cannot be rejected for all exchange rate series. This is consistent with the Nelson and Plosser (1982) argument that most macroeconomic time series have a stochastic trend. For the price ratios series the data are less informative. Based on the test statistics reported in panel A of Table 2.2, and the critical values, the null hypothesis of a unit root is rejected for the United Kingdom, Belgium, and Japan, in the case of the ADF test, and for the United Kingdom, France, Italy, Japan, Finland, Ireland, and Spain in the case of the PP test. Since the data on the price ratios are not very informative regarding the existence of a unit root for some of the series, for the testing I assume that all series have at least one unit root. In this respect the results for the United Kingdom and Japan should be interpreted with caution.

The tests for unit roots on the first differences of the log levels are not very informative for some of the series as well, as we can see from the results in panel B of Tables 2.1 and 2.2. Although with the PP test all series are found to be integrated of order one, using the ADF test some of the first differenced log levels appear to be non-stationary. It is unlikely that these macroeconomic series would have a higher order of integration than one, thus the decision here is to assume that all series are I(1).

2.3.2 COINTEGRATION TESTS

As mentioned by King and Watson (1997), long-run multiplier tests are inefficient in the presence of cointegration. To test the null hypothesis of no cointegration (against the alternative of cointegration) I use the Engle and Granger (1987) two-step procedure. This involves regressing one variable against the other to obtain the (OLS) residuals $\hat{e}$.

$$s_t = \beta_0 + \beta_1 t + \beta_2 p_t + \hat{e}_t. \quad (2.3.4)$$

A test of the null of no cointegration (against the alternative of cointegration) is based on testing for a unit root in the regression residuals $\hat{e}$. For this testing I use both an ADF and a PP test. Then I redo the testing using in (2.3.4) p_t as the dependent variable.

Table 2.3 summarizes the cointegration tests and reports the test statistics for the ADF test in panel A, and the PP test in panel B. The number of augmenting lags is chosen as discussed before. Based on these test statistics and the critical values at the 5% significance level, I conclude that the exchange rate and the price ratio do not cointegrate for all countries. Only for the case of Japan when p is used as the dependent variable there is evidence of cointegration but the null of no cointegration is accepted when p is the dependent variable.

Hence, the conditions necessary for the long-run multiplier tests to be meaningful [that is, exchange rate and price ratio series are I(1) and do not cointegrate] hold for all countries while the results for the United Kingdom and Japan should be interpreted with caution.

2.4 THE FISHER AND SEATER METHODOLOGY

Important macroeconomic hypotheses are dealing with the long run effects of some variables to other variables. The neutrality and superneutrality of money as well as the long run Phillips curve are some examples. In this paper, I examine the long run properties of PPP. I want to test whether changes in the relative price levels have an one to one effect on the nominal exchange rate.

Testing such hypotheses proved not to be trivial. Lucas (1972) and Sargent (1971) give examples where it is impossible to test long-run neutrality using reduced form econometric methods. In their examples they use rational expectations, short-run non-neutrality and stationary variables. The effect of using such variables is that these data can not be used to test for long-run neutrality since they do not sustain changes that are necessary for long-run effects. Lucas and Sargent with respect to this problem concluded that in order to test for long-run relationships it is important to construct complete behavioral models. Building on these arguments McCallum (1984) showed that low frequency band spectral estimators calculated using reduced form models suffered from the same problems that Lucas and Sargent exposed. In general, economists have not yet reached a consensus on the various long-run propositions. This of course is the result of the disagreement on the appropriate behavioral model for such research.

The results of the Lucas and Sargent critique are mainly driven from the stationarity property of the model's variables. In models where the variables are not stationary and follow integrated processes we can test the long-run properties without identifying a complete behavioral model. This is concluded in Sargent (1971) and it is discussed in detail in Fisher and Seater (1993). Even with non-stationary variables, long-run neutrality cannot be tested using a reduced form model. We must use the model's "final form", which shows the response of the model's variables to structural shocks.

The econometric analysis of simultaneous equations models of the reduced form of a structural model cannot be identified econometrically. This is because we need a priori restrictions to identify the structural disturbances. I must clarify here what I mean by the different forms of the model. By the "reduced form" model I mean a set of regression equations in which each endogenous variable is expressed as a function of lagged values of itself and other exogenous variables. By "final form" I mean a set of equations where the endogenous variables are a function of current and lagged values of shocks and exogenous variables. Finally, by "structural model" I mean a set of simultaneous equations where the endogenous variables are a function of other endogenous variables, exogenous variables, lags of the variables and structural disturbances[2].

2.4.1   THE LONG-RUN DERIVATIVE

Fisher and Seater (1993), define the long-run neutrality (LRN) and long-run superneutrality (LRSN) propositions in terms of a bivariate ARIMA model and use it to provide evidence on the LRN and LRSN properties of money.

---

[2] See also Geweke (1986), Stock & Watson (1988), King, Plosser, Stock & Watson (1991) and Gali (1992).

Here I will use the same methodology to test the long-run Purchasing Power Parity assumption. In particular, I am going to test whether exogenous permanent changes in the price ratio have a one-to-one permanent effect on the spot exchange rate.

Because PPP is a relationship that it is assumed to hold in the long-run, it does not depend on the short-run dynamics and structure of the economy. Thus, we can use tests for PPP that are structure-free. In doing this, the integration properties of the price ratio and the spot exchange rate will be very important.

Following Fisher and Seater (1993), I use a bivariate, stationary ARIMA representation:

$$a(L)\Delta^{<p>}p_t = b(L)\Delta^{<s>}s_t + u_t \qquad (2.4.1)$$

$$d(L)\Delta^{<s>}s_t = c(L)\Delta^{<p>}p_t + w_t \qquad (2.4.2)$$

where $p_t = \ln(P_t / P_t^*)$ and $s_t = \ln(S_t)$. P_t is the domestic price level at time period t and P_t^* is the foreign price level. Let $\Delta \equiv (1-L)$. $<x>$ represents the order of integration of variable x, so that if x is $I(\gamma)$ according to the terminology of Engle and Granger (1987), then $<x>=\gamma$ and also $<\Delta x>=<x>-1$. I restrict $a_0 = d_0 = 1$, and b_0 and c_0 are not restricted. The errors u_t and w_t are assumed to be independently and identically distributed with mean zero and variances σ_u^2 and σ_w^2, respectively.

When both the exchange rate and the price ratio are integrated of order one and $<s>=<p>=1$, the long-run derivative of s with respect to p can be written as:

$$LRD_{s,p} = \lim_{k \to \infty} \frac{\partial s_{t+k} / \partial u_t}{\partial p_{t+k} / \partial u_t}, \qquad (2.4.3)$$

if $\lim_{k \to \infty} \partial p_{t+k} / \partial u_t \neq 0$. If $\lim_{k \to \infty} \partial p_{t+k} / \partial u_t = 0$ then there are no permanent changes to the

price ratio and the long-run response of the exchange rate to a permanent change in the

price ratio is not defined. The sequence in the numerator measures the effect through time

of an exogenous price change and the sequence in the denominator measures the effect of

the exogenous change on the price ratio itself. So the LRD measures the long-run elasticity

of the exchange rate with respect to the price ratio. Thus, if PPP holds in the long-run, I

expect that $LRD_{s,p} = 1$. According to Fisher and Seater (1993), from the solution of

(2.4.1)-(2.4.2) we have:

$$\alpha(L) = d(L) / [a(L)d(L) - b(L)c(L)]$$

$$\gamma(L) = c(L) / [a(L)d(L) - b(L)c(L)].$$

Thus, we can evaluate the limits as:

$$\lim_{k \to \infty} \partial p_{t+k} / \partial u_t = \theta(1) ,$$

where $\theta(L) \equiv (1-L)^{1-<p>}\alpha(L)$. Similarly,

$$\lim_{k \to \infty} \partial s_{t+k} / \partial u_t = \Gamma(1),$$

where $\Gamma(L) \equiv (1-L)^{1-<s>}\gamma(L)$.

If the order of integration of the price ratio is not zero, then the LRD is defined and we can write:

$$LRD_{s,p} = \frac{(1-L)^{<p>-<s>}\gamma(L)|_{L=1}}{\alpha(1)} \qquad (2.4.4)$$

From (2.4.4) we can see that the value of the LRD depends on the order of integration of the two variables. When $<p>-<s>\geq 1$, then $LRD_{s,p} = 0$. When $<p>-<s>=0$ then from the solution to (2.4.1) - (2.4.2) and (2.4.4) we have:

$$LRD_{s,p} = \gamma(1)/\alpha(1) = c(1)/d(1). \qquad (2.4.5)$$

2.4.2   TESTING FOR PPP USING THE LRD

The case where $<s>=<p>=1$, is a very interesting case because we can test PPP. Because both the price ratio and the spot exchange rate are integrated of order one, there are permanent changes to both s and p. In the case where $<s>=<p>=2$ we have permanent changes to the growth rates of both s and p. Equation (2.4.4) implies that

$LRD_{\Delta s,\Delta p} = LRD_{s,p}$. This is an interesting implication because it means that tests on how the growth rate of the price ratio affects the growth rate of the exchange rate can be directly interpreted as tests of how a permanent change to the level of the price ratio affects the level of the exchange rate. The important implication of this is that if we find empirical evidence that supports the assumption of *Relative PPP* it can be directly interpreted as evidence for *Absolute PPP* when $<s>=<p>=2$.

When we have permanent innovations in both the price ratio and the exchange rate, or in other words when $<s>=<p>=1$, Fisher and Seater show that the LRD is given by equation (2.4.5). In this case, PPP holds if $LRD_{s,p}=1$, so that an exogenous permanent change to the price ratio has a permanent effect on the exchange rate. Under the Fisher and Seater identification scheme with exogenous p, c(1)/d(1) can be interpreted as: $\lim_{k\to\infty} b_k$ where b_k is the coefficient from the equation:

$$\sum_{j=0}^{k}\Delta^{<s>} s_{t-j} = a_k + b_k\left[\sum_{j=0}^{k}\Delta^{<p>} p_{t-j}\right]+e_{kt}. \qquad (2.4.6)$$

where $<s>=<p>=1$. Equation (2.4.6) can also be written as:

$$\Delta s_t + \Delta s_{t-1} + ... + \Delta s_{t-k} = a_k + b_k(\Delta p_t + \Delta p_{t-1} + ... + \Delta p_{t-k})+e_{kt} \Rightarrow$$

24

$$s_t - s_{t-1} + s_{t-1} - s_{t-2} + \ldots + s_{t-k} - s_{t-k-1}$$
$$= a_k + b_k(p_t - p_{t-1} + p_{t-1} - p_{t-2} + \ldots + p_{t-k} + p_{t-k-1}) + e_{kt} \Rightarrow$$

$$s_t - s_{t-k-1} = a_k + b_k(p_t - p_{t-k-1}), \quad \text{for } k = 1, \ldots, K(2.4.7)$$

We can use the data to estimate equation (2.4.7) and obtain estimates of b_k for different values of k and construct the corresponding confidence band.

2.4.3 THE EMPIRICAL ESTIMATION

Estimating equation (2.4.7) for each of the 16 countries, and for values of k ranging from 1 to 30 as in Fisher and Seater (1993), I get the results that are shown in Figures 2.1 to 2.16. In each graph, on the horizontal axis we have k, the number of lags for the corresponding regression. On the vertical axis we have the coefficient of the relative price b_k, which is also the LRD_{sp}. For every estimate of b_k, I also graph the upper and lower values for the 95% confidence interval for b_k using Newey and West's (1987) procedure. These confidence intervals are constructed from a t-distribution with T/k degrees of freedom, where T is the number of observations. The degrees of freedom are T/k instead of T-k since this is the number of non-overlapping observations[3]. If long-run PPP holds, then b_k should be equal to 1. Thus, on the graph I also include the line for which $b_k = 1$.

---

[3] See, for example, Hansen and Hodrick (1980).

Hence, there is evidence that supports long-run PPP if the $b_k=1$ line is contained in the confidence bands for the different values of k.

According to the above, we can see from Figures 2.1 to 2.16 that the null hypothesis that $b_k = 1$, cannot be rejected for any $k \in [1, 30]$ for Belgium, Denmark, Greece, Italy, the Netherlands, Norway, Spain, and Switzerland. Thus, I find strong evidence that PPP holds for these countries in the floating exchange rate period. For Austria, $b_k = 1$ can not be rejected for $1 \leq k \leq 20$ for higher values of k I reject the null. For Finland the null is only rejected for $20 \leq k \leq 27$, for Germany it is rejected for $k \geq 24$, for Ireland and Japan is rejected only for $6 \leq k \leq 12$ and $17 \leq k \leq 21$ respectively. For the U.K. the null is rejected for $17 \leq k \leq 27$. Finally for the case of Canada and France, we reject the null that $b_k = 1$, for almost all k.

Hence, from these results I conclude that there is evidence that PPP holds for all countries investigated with the exception of Canada and France.

2.5 THE KING & WATSON METHODOLOGY

In this section, I use the reduced form of the model under different a priori assumptions that identify the model and I pay attention to the long-run properties of the model under each identifying assumption. I identify the model using a wide range of assumptions in order to see the sensitivity of the results to the identifying assumptions. The robustness of the results to different sample periods is also investigated. I present the results both numerically and graphically.

2.5.1 ECONOMETRIC ISSUES

Consider a model which is linear in both the observed variables and the structural shocks. In particular, if the first differences of the nominal exchange rate and the relative price level are stationary the model's final form can be written as:

$$\Delta s_t = \mu_s + \theta_{s\eta}(L)\varepsilon_t^\eta + \theta_{sp}(L)\varepsilon_t^p \qquad (2.5.1)$$

$$\Delta p_t = \mu_p + \theta_{p\eta}(L)\varepsilon_t^\eta + \theta_{pp}(L)\varepsilon_t^p \qquad (2.5.2)$$

where ε_t^η is a vector of shocks other than the relative price level that affects the nominal exchange rate. ε_t^p is a shock that permanently affects the price level (relative). And also, the other terms are defined similarly to (2.5.3).

$$\theta_{pp}(L)\varepsilon_t^p = \sum \theta_{pp}^j \varepsilon_{t-j}^p \quad (2.5.3)$$

The lag polynomials $\theta_{s\eta}(L)$, $\theta_{sp}(L)$, $\theta_{p\eta}(L)$ and $\theta_{pp}(L)$ incorporate the rich dynamics of the model. The long-run test of PPP that I want to conduct is summarized in the question: does an unexpected and permanent change in the relative price level p, cause a permanent one-for-one change to the nominal exchange rate s? If yes, then the Purchasing Power Parity assumption holds in the long-run. In equations (2.5.1) and (2.5.2) ε_t^p is the exogenous change in the price level. Thus, the permanent effect of ε_t^p to the price level will be: $\sum \theta_{pp}^j \varepsilon_t^P = \theta_{pp}(1)\varepsilon_t^P$. Similarly, the permanent effect of ε_t^P to the nominal exchange rate will be: $\sum \theta_{sp}^j \varepsilon_t^P = \theta_{sp}(1)\varepsilon_t^P$. Thus, the long run elasticity of the nominal exchange rate with respect to permanent exogenous change in the price level is:

$$\gamma_{sp} = \frac{\theta_{sp}(1)}{\theta_{pp}(1)}. \qquad (2.5.4)$$

Thus, if PPP holds, $\gamma_{sp} = 1$. This means that the permanent shock to the relative price level has a permanent long-run effect on the nominal exchange rate. It is important to note here that we can test this long-run property that $\gamma_{sp} = 1$ only when the price level variable is not stationary. The reason is that if the relative price level is stationary, a shock to the price level has no permanent effect in the level of p and so $\theta_{pp}(1) = 0$. In this case, the long-run elasticity of equation (2.5.4) is not defined. This is why Lucas and Sargent reached the conclusion that we need a complete behavioral model to test the long-run neutrality of money. In the case of money, we want to test whether permanent changes in the money supply will have a permanent effect on output. Of course, if the data for the money supply are stationary and there are no permanent changes, we cannot use these data to test for long-run neutrality. For the case of the long-run PPP, if there are no permanent changes in the historical data of the relative price level, I cannot use these data to test for the effects of a permanent change in the price level to the exchange rate. On the other hand, if the relative price level is not stationary and it contains a unit root, then $\theta_{pp}(1) \neq 0$ and the long-run elasticity of equation (2.5.4) is well defined.

2.5.2   THE KING AND WATSON TESTING PROCEDURE

The reduced form of the model as it is described by equations (2.5.1) and (2.5.2) cannot be used to estimate the parameters using available data. I must first address econometric identification issues. King and Watson, approach this problem in an "unusual" way. Rather than using an a priori set of identifying assumptions and solve for the model's parameters, they employ an eclectic approach. They investigate the long-run relationships by imposing a wide range of identifying restrictions. This approach provides evidence of the robustness of any conclusion to different identifying assumptions.

First, I assume that $(\varepsilon_t^\eta, \varepsilon_t^p)$ is a vector of unobserved mean zero and serially independent random variables such that equations (2.5.1) and (2.5.2) can be interpreted as vector moving average model. The estimation strategy begins by inverting the moving average model to form a vector autoregressive model (VAR). The VAR which is assumed to be of finite order is then analyzed as dynamic linear simultaneous equations model[4].

The estimation using this procedure requires two additional sets of assumptions. The first, in order to transform the vector moving average model into a VAR and the second to econometrically identify the parameters of the VAR. These two sets of assumptions are closely related: the moving average model can only be inverted if the VAR includes enough

---

[4] See Blanchard and Watson (1986), Bernanke (1986), Sims (1986) and also Watson (1994) for a survey.

variables to reconstruct the structural shocks. Thus, if $(\varepsilon_t^{\eta}, \varepsilon_t^{p})$ is an n x 1 vector, then there must be n variables in the VAR. But the identification of an n-variable VAR requires n x (n-1) a priori restrictions. This means that the necessary number of identifying restrictions increases with the square of the number of structural shocks. King and Watson assume that n = 2, so that only bivariate VAR's are required. This is a fairly standard assumption and it is employed by many other researchers in the study of neutrality propositions. This also helps tractability: when n = 2 then only 2 identifying restrictions are necessary. The drawback of this approach is that some of the results may be contaminated by omitted variables bias.

To derive the set of observationally equivalent models, let $X_t = (\Delta s_t \ \Delta p_t)$ and so equations (2.5.1)-(2.5.2) become:

$$X_t = \theta(L)\varepsilon_t, \qquad (2.5.5)$$

where $\varepsilon_t = (\varepsilon_t^{\eta} \ \varepsilon_t^{p})$ represents the 2 x 1 vector of structural disturbances. Assume that $|\theta(z)|$ has all of its zeros outside the unit circle so that we can invert to obtain the VAR:

$$\alpha(L)X_t = \varepsilon_t \qquad (2.5.6)$$

where $\alpha(L) = \sum_{j=0}^{\infty} \alpha^j L^j$ with α^j a 2 x 2 matrix. It is important here to note that since the

invertibility of (L) requires that (1) has a full rank, this implies that s_t and p_t are both

integrated processes and that they are not cointegrated. Unstacking the matrix form model

I get:

$$\Delta s_t = \lambda_{sp} \Delta p_t + \sum_{j=1}^{k} a_{sp}^j \Delta p_{t-j} + \sum_{j=1}^{k} a_{ss}^j \Delta s_{t-j} + \varepsilon_t^s \qquad (2.5.7)$$

$$\Delta p_t = \lambda_{ps} \Delta s_t + \sum_{j=1}^{k} a_{pp}^j \Delta p_{t-j} + \sum_{j=1}^{k} a_{ps}^j \Delta s_{t-j} + \varepsilon_t^p \qquad (2.5.8)$$

which is written under the assumption that the VAR in equation (2.5.6) is of order k.

Equations (2.5.7)-(2.5.8) are a set of dynamic simultaneous equations. If $\Sigma_\varepsilon = E(\varepsilon_t \varepsilon_t')$,

then the reduced form of (2.5.6) is:

$$X_t = \sum_{i=1}^{k} \Phi_i X_{t-i} + e_t \qquad (2.5.9)$$

where $\Phi_i = -\alpha_0^{-1} \alpha_i$ and $e_t = \alpha_0^{-1} \varepsilon_t$. The matrices α_i and Σ_ε are determined by the set of

equations:

$$\alpha_0^{-1} \alpha_i = -\Phi_i, \quad i = 1,...k \qquad (2.5.10)$$

$$\alpha_0^{-1} \Sigma_\varepsilon \alpha_0^{-1} = \Sigma_e = E(e_t e_t'). \qquad (2.5.11)$$

When there are no restrictions on coefficients on lags in equation (2.5.9), equation (2.5.10) imposes no restrictions on α_0. It serves to determine α_i as a function of α_0 and Φ_i. Equation (2.5.11) determines both α_0 and Σ_ε as a function of Σ_e. Since Σ_e (a 2 x 2 symmetric matrix) has only three unique elements, only three unknown parameters in α_0 and Σ_ε can be identified. Equations (2.5.7)-(2.5.8) place 1's on the diagonal of α_0, but only three of the remaining parameters $\text{var}(\varepsilon_t^p)$, $\text{var}(\varepsilon_t^s)$, $\text{cov}(\varepsilon_t^p, \varepsilon_t^s)$, λ_{ps} and λ_{sp} can be identified. Following the standard practice in structural VAR analysis I assume that the structural shocks are not correlated. I place no restriction on the contemporaneous correlation of s and p so non-zero values for λ_{ps} and λ_{sp} allow both s and p to respond to ε^p and ε^s shocks within the period. With the assumption that $\text{cov}(\varepsilon_t^p, \varepsilon_t^s) = 0$, only one additional identifying assumption is required in order to get the parameter estimates.

I can assume either that $\lambda_{ps} = 0$ or that $\lambda_{sp} = 0$. These assumptions would imply that there are no contemporaneous effects of the relative price level and the exchange rate to each other. I can assume that PPP holds, and set $\gamma_{sp} = 1$, or I can assume that $\gamma_{ps} = 0$ which is consistent with no long-run effect of the exchange rate to the relative price level.

Here, I employ the eclectic approach that King and Watson proposed, where instead of focusing on a single identifying restriction, I report results for a wide range of identifying restrictions. This approach is more informative in terms of the robustness of inference about the relationship between the relative price level and the nominal exchange rate. In particular

32

I iterate each of the parameters λ_{ps}, λ_{sp}, γ_{ps}, and γ_{sp} within a reasonable range each time obtaining estimates of the remaining three parameters and their standard errors. These standard errors then are used to construct confidence intervals for the estimated long-run elasticity γ_{sp}. This approach is similar to what Sims (1989) and Blanchard (1989) have used for robustness calculations in VAR models.

2.5.3   THE ESTIMATION PROCEDURE

Under each alternative identifying restriction, I construct the Gaussian maximum likelihood estimates using instrumental variable estimation.

When λ_{ps} is assumed known and it is used to identify the model, equation (2.5.8) can be estimated by ordinary least squares (OLS) by regressing:

$$\Delta p_t - \lambda_{ps} \Delta s_t \qquad \text{onto} \qquad \left\{ \Delta s_{t-i}, \Delta p_{t-i} \right\}_{i=1}^{k}$$

Then equation (2.5.7) cannot be estimated using OLS because one of the explanatory variables, Δp_t, is potentially contemporaneously correlated with the error term ε_t^s and the OLS estimates would be biased and inefficient. To overcome this potential problem I use instrumental variables and the instruments are: $\left\{ \Delta s_{t-i}, \Delta p_{t-i} \right\}_{i=1}^{k}$ and the residuals from the estimated equation (2.5.8). These residuals are appropriate as instruments because of the assumption that the residuals from the two equations are uncorrelated or $\text{cov}(\varepsilon_t^p, \varepsilon_t^s) = 0$.

The parameter of interest here is the long-run multiplier γ_{sp} and this is equal to:

$$\gamma_{sp} = \frac{a_{sp}(1)}{1-\beta_{ss}} \qquad (2.5.12)$$

where $a_{sp}(1) = \sum_{j=0}^{k} a_{sp}^{j}$ and $\beta_{ss} = \sum_{j=1}^{k} a_{ss}^{j}$.

When λ_{sp} is assumed known, I only have to estimate equation (2.5.7). This is because the parameter of interest is γ_{sp}. Using OLS I regress:

$$\Delta s_t - \lambda_{sp}\Delta p_t \qquad \text{onto} \qquad \left\{\Delta s_{t-i}, \Delta p_{t-i}\right\}_{i=1}^{k}.$$

Then γ_{sp} is calculated according to (2.5.12).

When a value for γ_{ps} is used to identify the model, I can use a similar procedure. First I rewrite equation (2.5.8) as:

$$\Delta p_t = a_{ps}(1)\Delta s_t + \beta_{pp}\Delta p_{t-1} + \sum_{j=0}^{k-1} \tilde{a}_{ps}^{j}\Delta^2 s_{t-j} + \sum_{j=1}^{k-1} \tilde{a}_{pp}^{j}\Delta^2 p_{t-j} + \varepsilon_t^{p} \qquad (2.5.13)$$

where $\beta_{pp} = \sum_{j=1}^{k} \alpha_{pp}^{j}$. Equation (2.5.13) replaces the regressors:

$$(\Delta s_{t}, \Delta s_{t-1}, \dots, \Delta s_{t-k}, \Delta p_{t-1}, \dots, \Delta p_{t-k})$$

in equation (2.5.8) with the set of equivalent regressors:

$$(\Delta s_{t}, \Delta p_{t-1}, \Delta^2 s_{t}, \Delta^2 s_{t-1}, \dots, \Delta^2 s_{t-k+1}, \Delta^2 p_{t-1}, \dots, \Delta^2 p_{t-k+1}).$$

In equation (2.5.13) the long-run multiplier is $\gamma_{ps} = \dfrac{\alpha_{ps}(1)}{1 - \beta_{pp}}$, so that $\alpha_{ps}(1) = \gamma_{ps} - \beta_{pp}\gamma_{ps}$

. Substituting this in equation (2.5.12) and rearranging I get:

$$\Delta p_{t} - \gamma_{ps}\Delta s_{t} = \beta_{pp}(\Delta p_{t-1} - \gamma_{ps}\Delta s_{t}) + \sum_{j=0}^{k-1}\alpha_{ps}^{j}\Delta^2 s_{t-j} + \sum_{j=1}^{k-1}\alpha_{pp}^{j}\Delta^2 p_{t-j} + \varepsilon_{t}^{p}.$$

$$(2.5.14)$$

Equation (2.5.14) can be estimated using instrumental variables by regressing:

$\Delta p_{t} - \gamma_{ps}\Delta s_{t}$ onto $(\Delta p_{t-1} - \gamma_{ps}\Delta s_{t}, \Delta^2 s_{t}, \Delta^2 s_{t-1}, \dots, \Delta^2 s_{t-k+1}, \Delta^2 p_{t-1}, \dots, \Delta^2 p_{t-k+1}),$

using $\left\{\Delta s_{t-i}, \Delta p_{t-i}\right\}_{i=1}^{k}$ as instruments. I use instrumental variables in order to address the issue of potential contemporaneous correlation between Δs_t and the error term.

Equation (2.5.7) can now be estimated by instrumental variables using the residuals of the estimated equation (2.5.14) with $\left\{\Delta s_{t-i}, \Delta p_{t-i}\right\}_{i=1}^{k}$.

When a value for γ_{sp} is used to identify the model, this process is reversed.

2.5.4 THE ESTIMATION RESULTS

Following the procedures described in the previous section, I use a wide range of identifying parameter restrictions on λ_{ps}, λ_{sp}, γ_{ps}, and γ_{sp}. Table 2.4 and Figures 2.17-2.32 summarize the results. Table 2.4 (columns 2-4) shows the point estimates for λ_{ps}, λ_{sp}, and γ_{ps} when I assume that PPP holds in the long-run, or equivalently when I impose $\gamma_{sp} = 1$. The numbers in the parentheses represent the corresponding standard errors. Columns 5-7, show the intervals for each identifying parameter values for which PPP is rejected at the 95% confidence level. In Figures 2.17-2.32, I present the point estimates and the 95% confidence bands for the long-run multiplier γ_{sp}, for a wide range of plausible values of the other three parameters. In panel A, I iterate values for λ_{ps}, the contemporaneous effect of the exchange rate on the relative price. In panel B, I use a range of plausible values for λ_{sp}, the contemporaneous effect of the relative price on the

36

exchange rate. Clearly if PPP held at all times instantly, then this parameter would be equal to 1, and if the relative price has no effect on the exchange rate it would be equal to 0. For the estimation I use a range of values of $-1 \leq \lambda_{sp} \leq 2$ to address even the case where the contemporaneous effect of the relative price to the exchange rate may be negative. Finally, in panel C, I iterate the values for the long-run multiplier of the exchange rate on the relative price, γ_{ps}. The range of values that are used is $-5 \leq \gamma_{ps} \leq 5$. The estimates of γ_{sp} and the corresponding confidence bands are shown for ranges of the identifying parameters that standard errors are relatively small and do not explode.

The results from Figures 2.17-2.32, suggest that there is evidence that PPP holds in the long-run for all 16 OECD countries that I test here, since their 95% confidence bands for γ_{sp} include the value 1 for all different values of the identifying restrictions presented in the graphs. The only exceptions for certain intervals, are Canada, Ireland and Norway: for Canada, the 95% confidence band of the long-run multiplier γ_{sp} does not include $\gamma_{sp} = 1$ for the range $0.2 \leq \lambda_{ps} \leq 0.3$ in panel A, and for the range $0.2 \leq \gamma_{ps} \leq 0.4$ in panel C. For Ireland, the 95% confidence band lies above $\gamma_{sp} = 1$ for $-0.7 \leq \lambda_{ps} \leq -0.2$ in panel A and $\gamma_{ps} \leq -0.7$ in panel C. Finally for Norway the values for which PPP is rejected in the long-run is for $\lambda_{ps} = 0.1$ in panel A and the interval $0.3 \leq \gamma_{ps} \leq 0.4$ in panel C.

2.6 CONCLUSIONS

In this paper I have tested for PPP, the hypothesis that a change in the relative prices between two countries has a one-for-one effect on the exchange rate. I used quarterly data

Figure 2.5. LRD for Finland

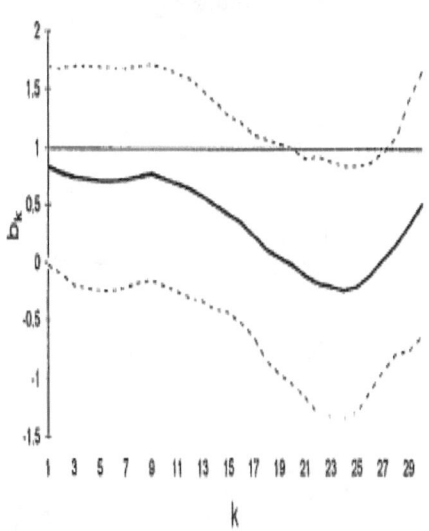

Figure 2.6. LRD for France

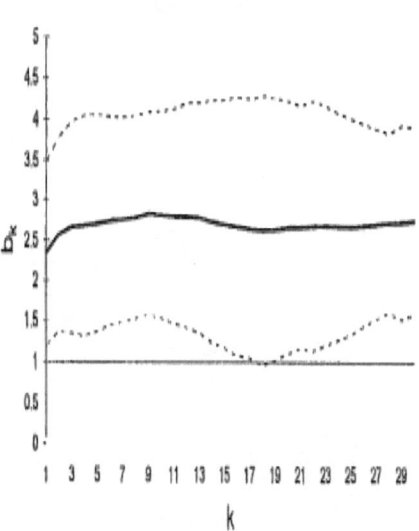

Figure 2.7. LRD for Germany

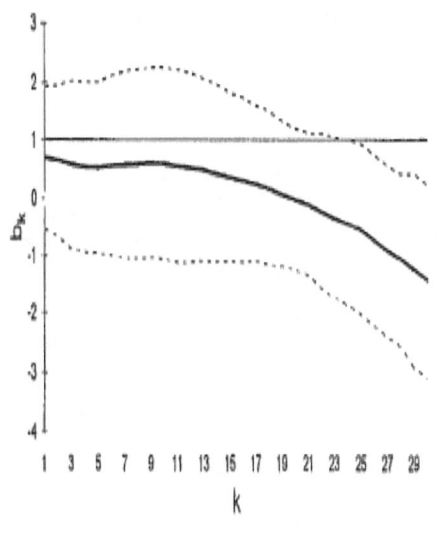

Figure 2.8. LRD for Greece

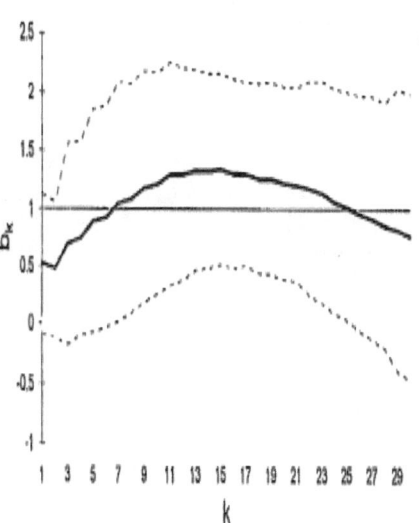

Figure 2.9. LRD for Ireland

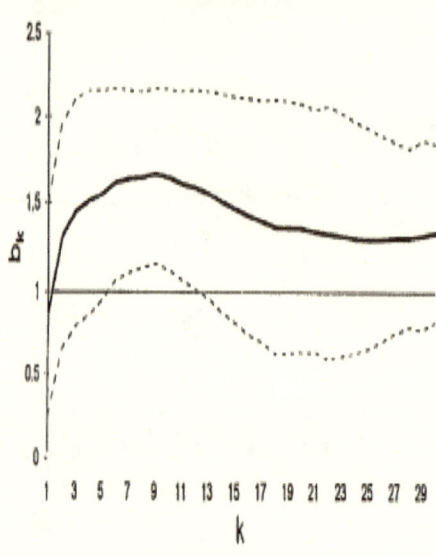

Figure 2.10. LRD for Italy

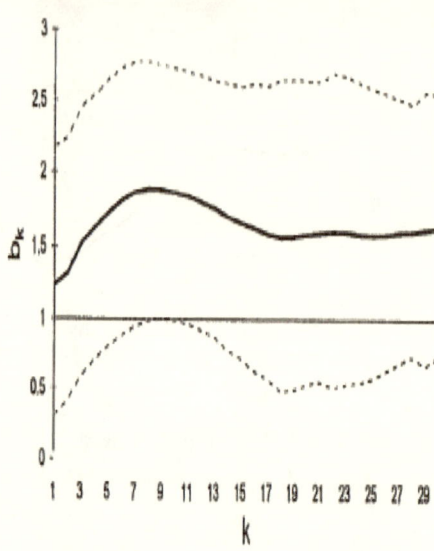

Figure 2.11. LRD for Japan

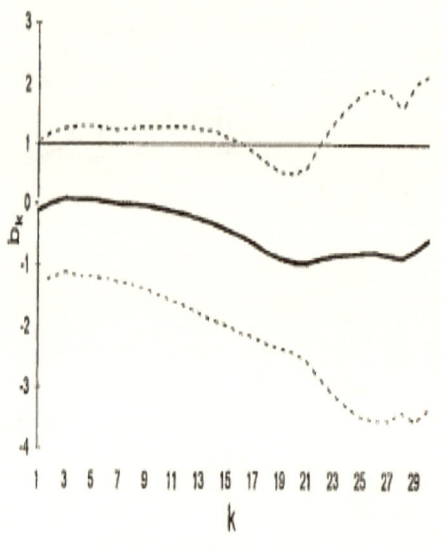

Figure 2.12. LRD for the Netherlands

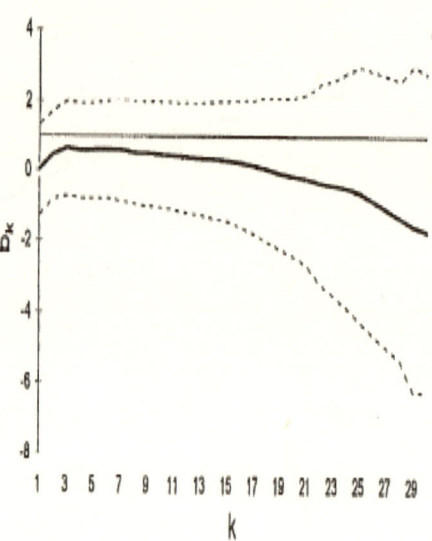

Figure 2.13. LRD for Norway

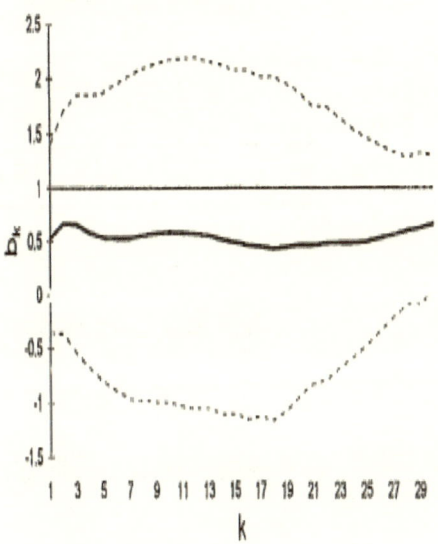

Figure 2.14. LRD for Spain

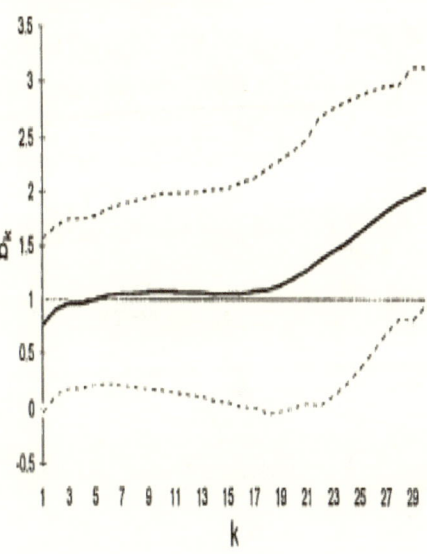

Figure 2.15. LRD for Switzerland

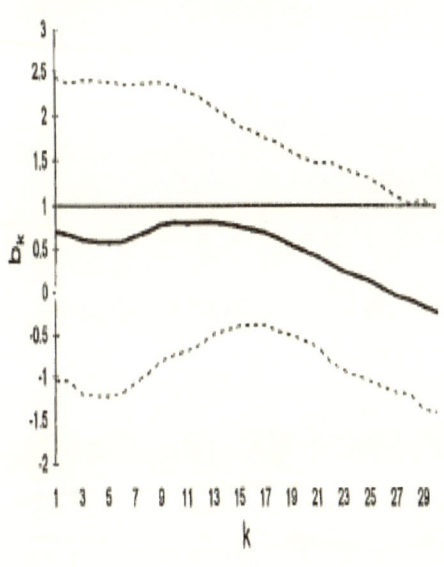

Figure 2.16. LRD for the U.K.

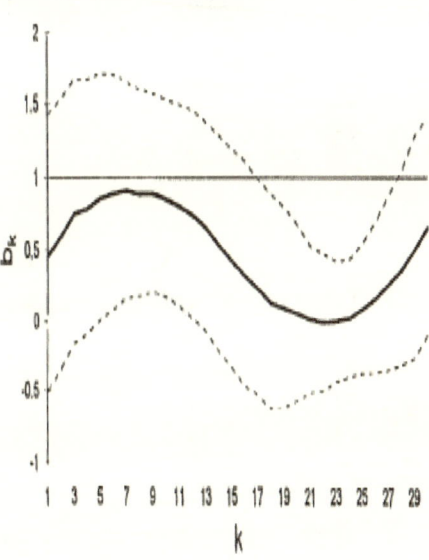

Figure 2.17. PPP Tests for Austria

A. 95% Confidence intervals for γ_{sp} as a function of λ_{ps}

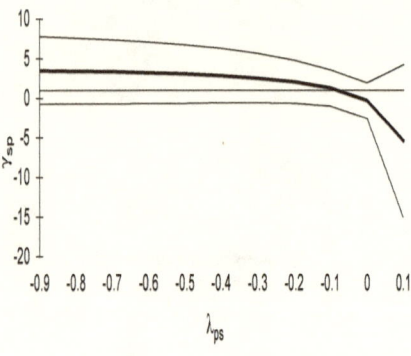

B. 95% Confidence intervals for γ_{sp} as a function of λ_{sp}

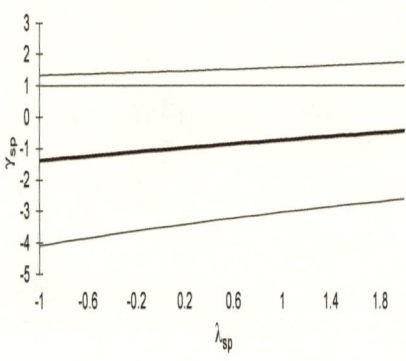

C. 95% Confidence intervals for γ_{sp} as a function of γ_{ps}

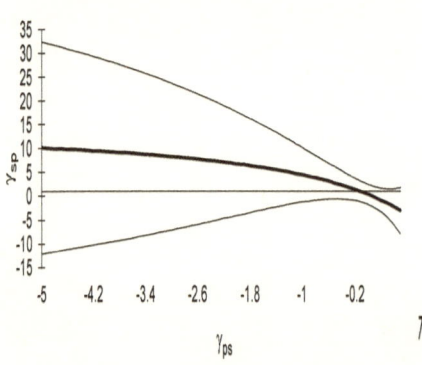

Figure 2.18. PPP Tests for Belgium

A. 95% Confidence intervals for γ_{sp} as a function of λ_{ps}

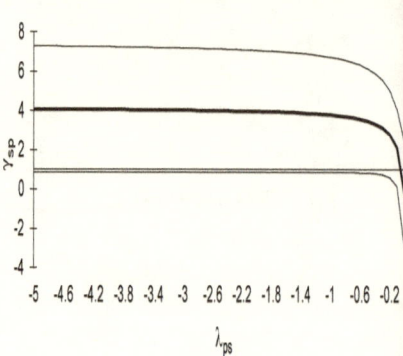

B. 95% Confidence intervals for γ_{sp} as a function of λ_{sp}

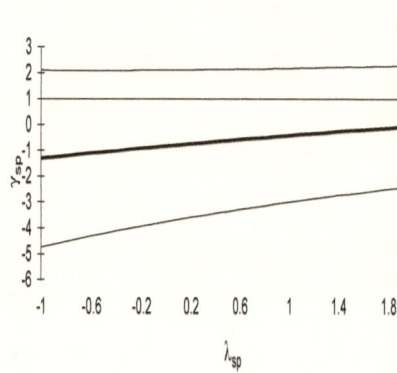

C. 95% Confidence intervals for γ_{sp} as a function of γ_{ps}

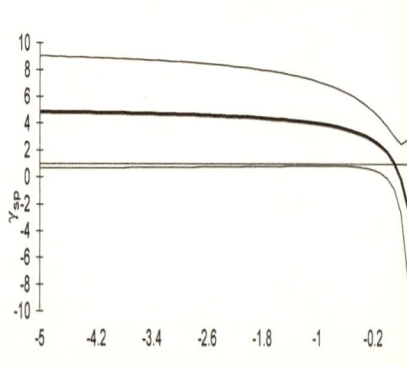

7

Figure 2.19. PPP Tests for Canada

A. 95% Confidence intervals for γ_{sp} as a function of λ_{ps}

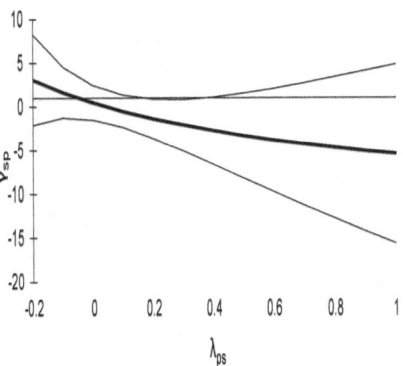

B. 95% Confidence intervals for γ_{sp} as a function of λ_{sp}

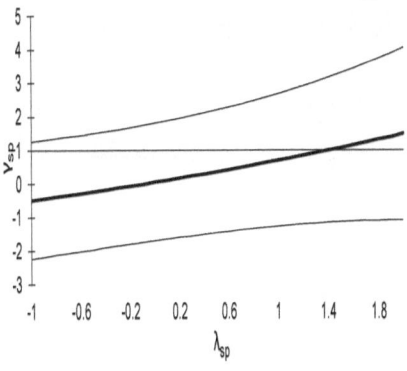

C. 95% Confidence intervals for γ_{sp} as a function of γ_{ps}

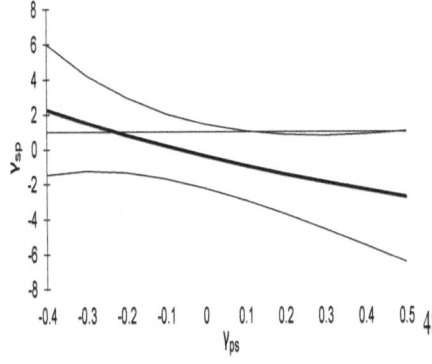

Figure 2.20. PPP Tests for Denmark

A. 95% Confidence intervals for γ_{sp} as a function of λ_{ps}

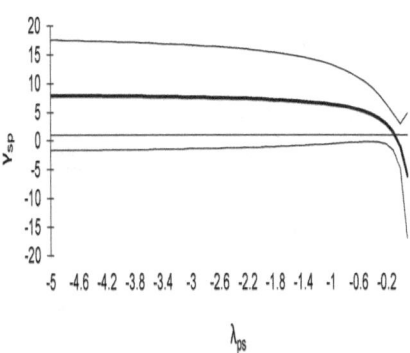

B. 95% Confidence intervals for γ_{sp} as a function of λ_{sp}

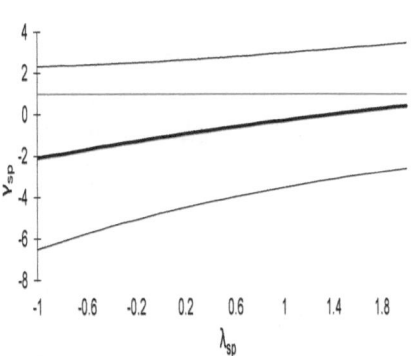

C. 95% Confidence intervals for γ_{sp} as a function of γ_{ps}

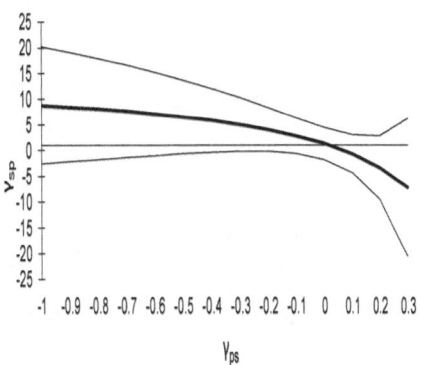

Figure 2.21. PPP Tests for Finland

A. 95% Confidence intervals for γ_{sp} as a function of λ_{ps}

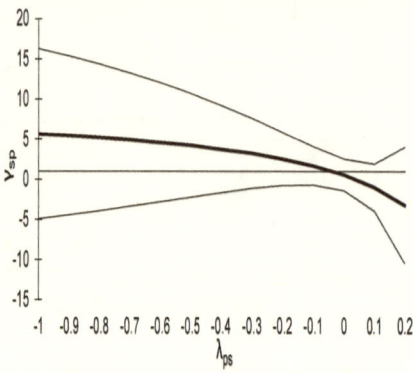

B. 95% Confidence intervals for γ_{sp} as a function of λ_{sp}

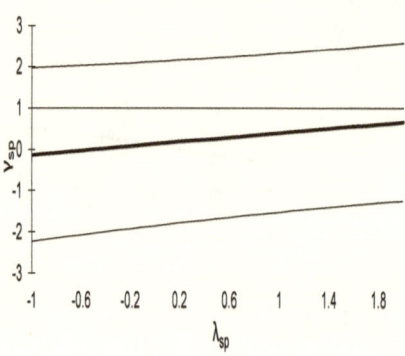

C. 95% Confidence intervals for γ_{sp} as a function of γ_{ps}

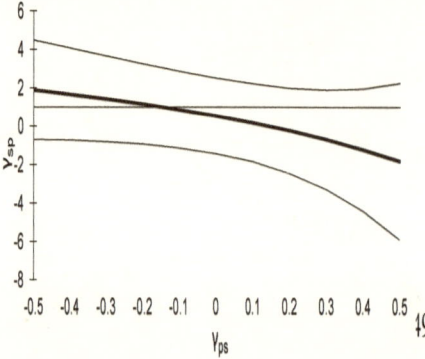

Figure 2.22. PPP Tests for France

A. 95% Confidence intervals for γ_{sp} as a function of λ_{ps}

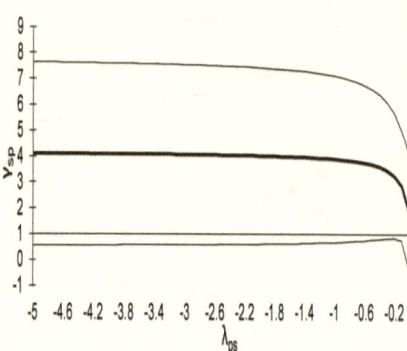

B. 95% Confidence intervals for γ_{sp} as a function of λ_{sp}

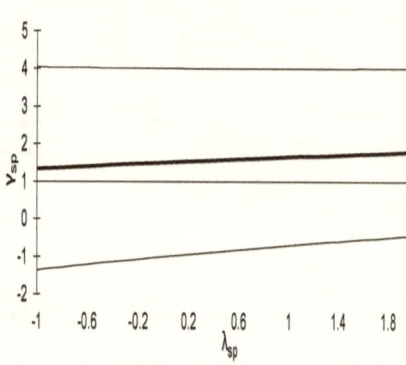

C. 95% Confidence intervals for γ_{sp} as a function of γ_{ps}

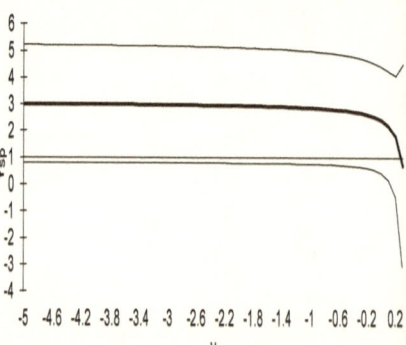

49

Figure 2.23. PPP Tests for Germany

A. 95% Confidence intervals for γ_{sp} as a function of λ_{ps}

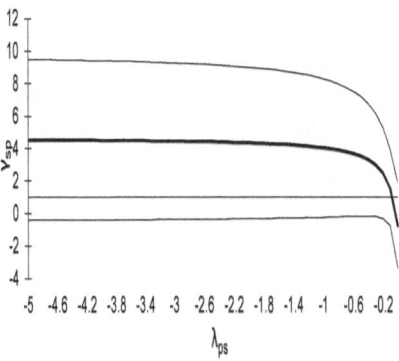

B. 95% Confidence intervals for γ_{sp} as a function of λ_{sp}

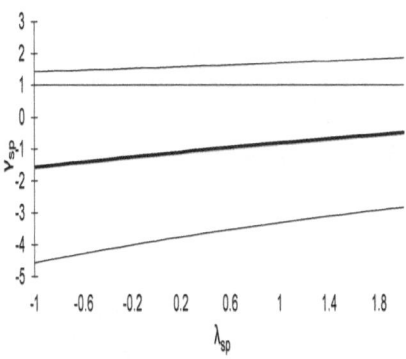

C. 95% Confidence intervals for γ_{sp} as a function of γ_{ps}

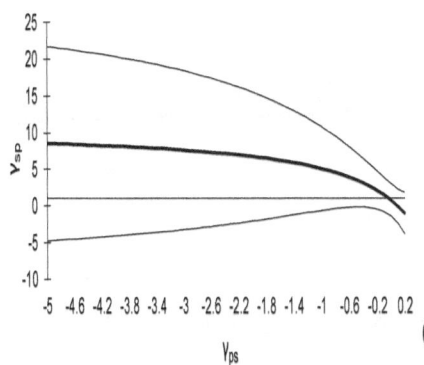

Figure 2.24. PPP Tests for Greece

A. 95% Confidence intervals for γ_{sp} as a function of λ_{ps}

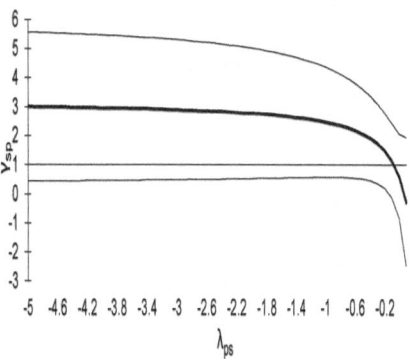

B. 95% Confidence intervals for γ_{sp} as a function of λ_{sp}

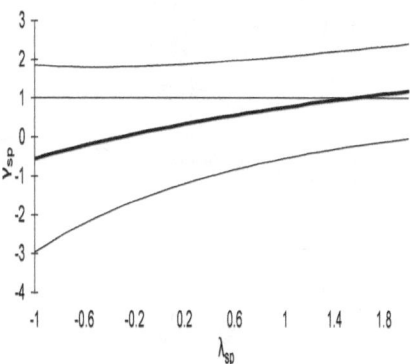

C. 95% Confidence intervals for γ_{sp} as a function of γ_{ps}

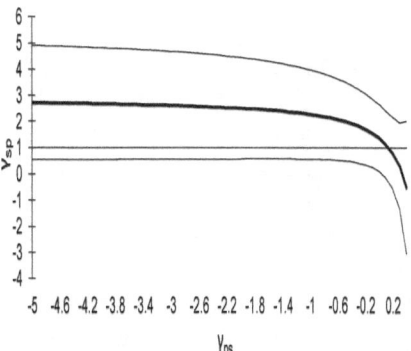

0

Figure 2.25. PPP Tests for Ireland

A. 95% Confidence intervals for γ_{sp} as a function of λ_{ps}

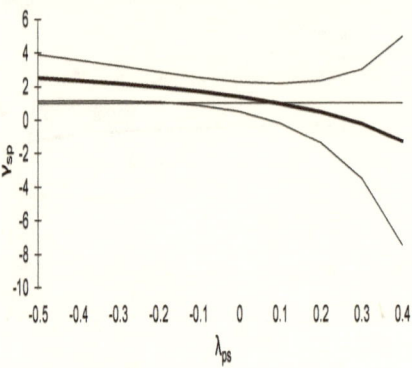

B. 95% Confidence intervals for γ_{sp} as a function of λ_{sp}

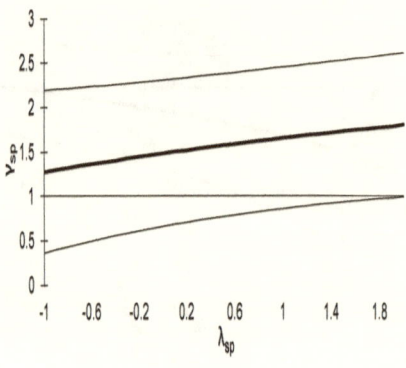

C. 95% Confidence intervals for γ_{sp} as a function of γ_{ps}

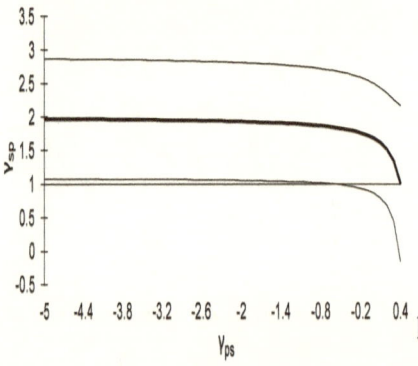

Figure 2.26. PPP Tests for Italy

A. 95% Confidence intervals for γ_{sp} as a function of λ_{ps}

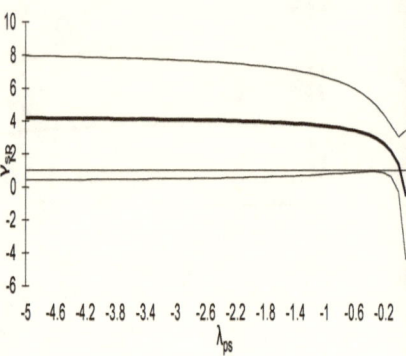

B. 95% Confidence intervals for γ_{sp} as a function of λ_{sp}

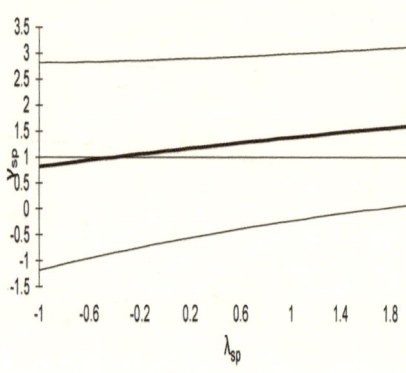

C. 95% Confidence intervals for γ_{sp} as a function of γ_{ps}

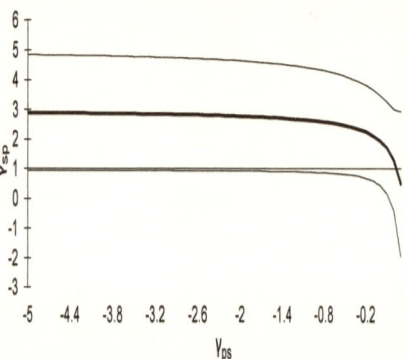

1

Figure 2.27. PPP Tests for Japan

A. 95% Confidence intervals for γ_{sp} as a function of λ_{ps}

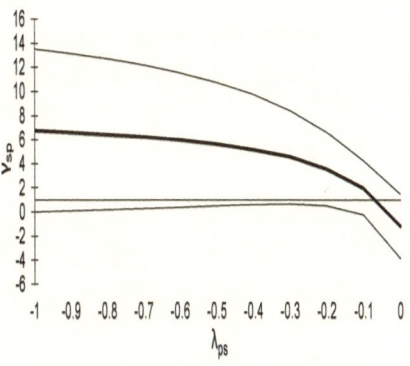

B. 95% Confidence intervals for γ_{sp} as a function of λ_{sp}

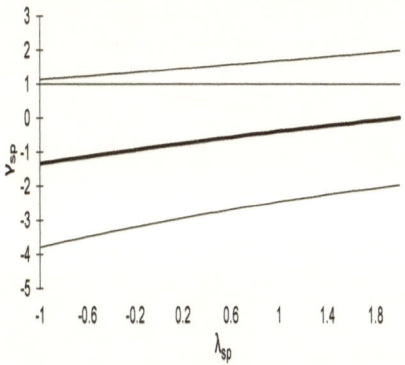

C. 95% Confidence intervals for γ_{sp} as a function of γ_{ps}

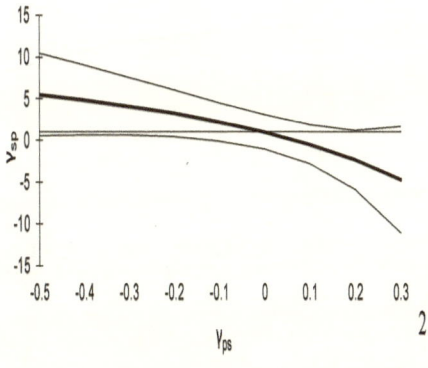

Figure 2.28. PPP Tests for Netherlands

A. 95% Confidence intervals for γ_{sp} as a function of λ_{ps}

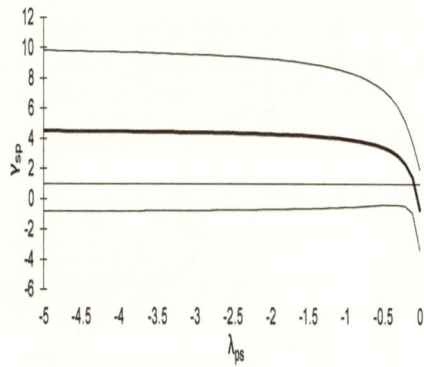

B. 95% Confidence intervals for γ_{sp} as a function of λ_{sp}

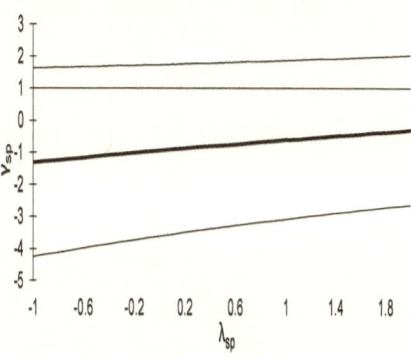

C. 95% Confidence intervals for γ_{sp} as a function of γ_{ps}

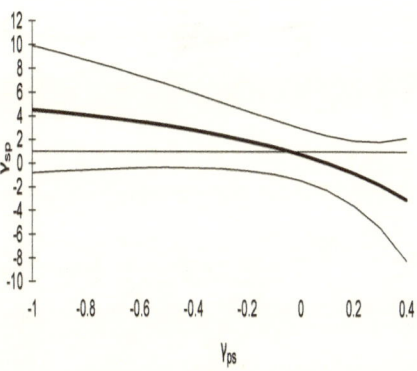

A. 95% Confidence intervals for γ_{sp} as a function of λ_{ps}

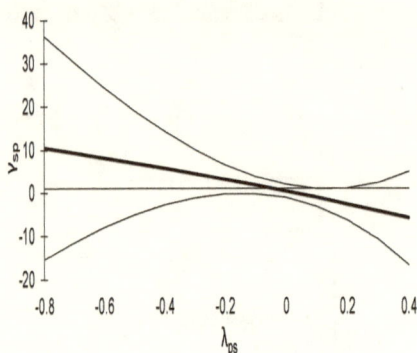

A. 95% Confidence intervals for γ_{sp} as a function of λ_{ps}

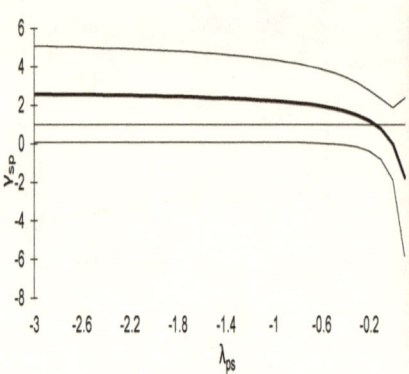

B. 95% Confidence intervals for γ_{sp} as a function of λ_{sp}

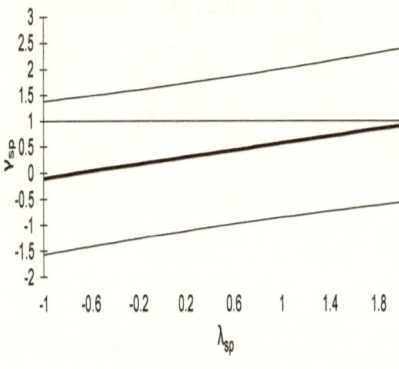

B. 95% Confidence intervals for γ_{sp} as a function of λ_{sp}

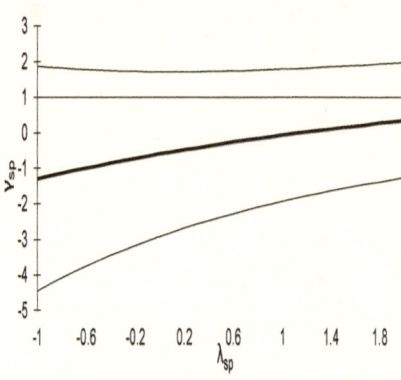

C. 95% Confidence intervals for γ_{sp} as a function of γ_{ps}

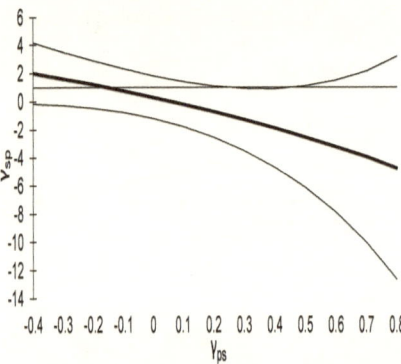

C. 95% Confidence intervals for γ_{sp} as a function of γ_{ps}

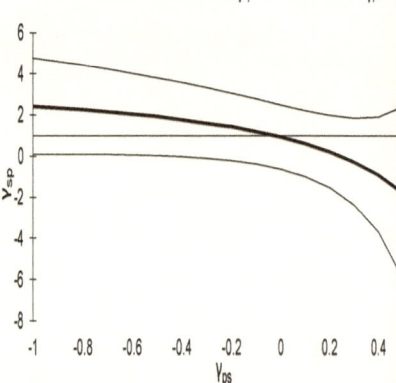

Figure 2.31. PPP Tests for Switzerland

A. 95% Confidence intervals for γ_{sp} as a function of $\hat{\lambda}_{ps}$

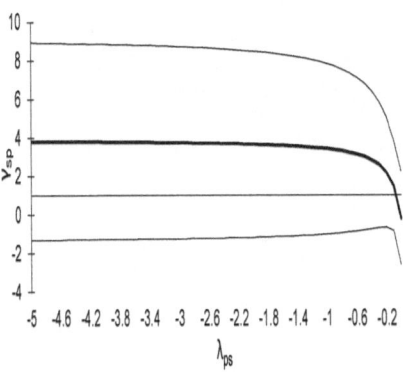

B. 95% Confidence intervals for γ_{sp} as a function of $\hat{\lambda}_{sp}$

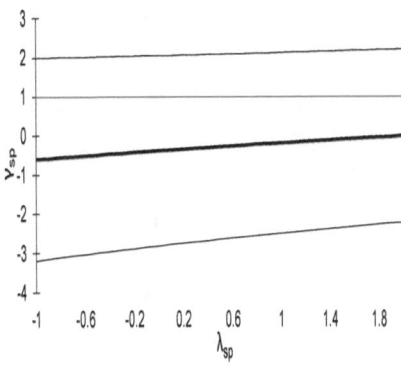

C. 95% Confidence intervals for γ_{sp} as a function of $\hat{\gamma}_{ps}$

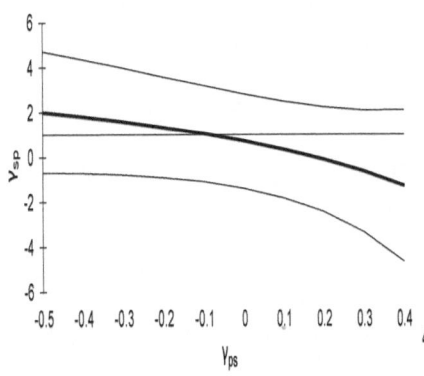

Figure 2.32. PPP Tests for the U.K.

A. 95% Confidence intervals for γ_{sp} as a function of $\hat{\lambda}_{ps}$

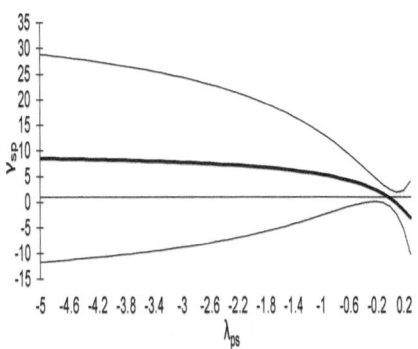

B. 95% Confidence intervals for γ_{sp} as a function of $\hat{\lambda}_{sp}$

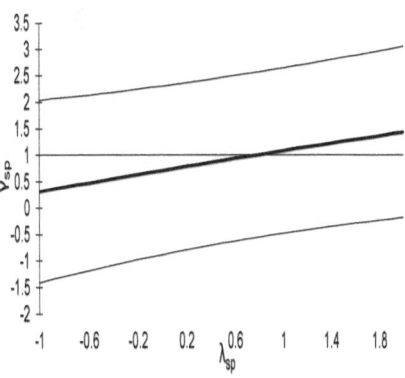

C. 95% Confidence intervals for γ_{sp} as a function of γ_{ps}

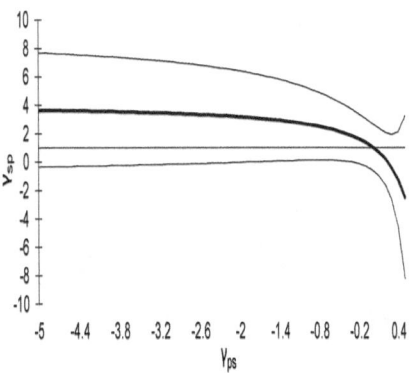

4

CHAPTER 3

MODELLING AND FORECASTING VOLATILITY

IN ENERGY MARKET FUTURES

3.1 INTRODUCTION

The conventional econometric models that are used to describe the evolution of a time series over time and to produce reliable forecasts for the future assume that the variance of the series in question is constant over time, or in other words that the errors are homoskedastic. Many economic time series do not demonstrate a constant variance over time, but we observe volatility clustering, periods during which volatility is relatively high and other periods where volatility is low. Traditional econometric modeling and forecasting techniques would estimate the variance from the sample in hand and use it to describe the properties of the time series in question as well as for producing forecasts. Recent developments in the field of econometrics allow us to distinguish between the unconditional and the conditional variance of a time series. The unconditional variance refers to the population variance or the variance of the whole sample in hand, while the conditional variance depends on past realizations of shocks that are known at the present period.

In many cases it is important to be able to forecast the conditional variance of a series. For example, when an investor is trying to decide whether or not to hold an asset for one period, she is interested in both the expected rate of return of the asset and its expected variance in order to optimize her portfolio. In this case the unconditional variance-i.e. the population variance of the series-is of little importance to her if she plans to hold the asset for only one period. The conditional variance, based on the information set Ω_t which includes the past realizations of the conditional variance and prices will be more appropriate for this decision. Models that use the conditional variance for estimation and forecasts, can better take into account the observed heteroskedasticity and other non-linear processes in the error term.

In recent years, the most important innovation in modeling the volatility in economic time series, was the work by Engle (1982) who introduced the autoregressive conditional heteroskedasticity or ARCH, to model the conditional variance.

In this paper I use the Box-Jenkins methodology to model the time series properties of six energy market futures prices. These are crude oil, electricity, heating oil, natural gas, propane, and unleaded gas. These series are characterized by periods of high volatility and periods of relative tranquility as it is shown below, which is typical of ARCH processes in the error structure. Thus, I also employ and compare the ARCH, GARCH, ARCH-M, and EGARCH methodologies introduced by Engle (1982), Bollerslev (1986), Engle, Lilien and Robins (1987), and Nelson (1991) respectively in order to model the conditional variance of the series. These models are then used for in-sample forecasts of the mean and the conditional variance for each of the six series.

In section 2 I describe the data that are used in this paper, in section 3 I discuss the methodology that will be used, in section 4 is the empirical estimation of the best fitted models, in section 5 I produce in-sample forecasts for the six series and finally in section 6 I conclude.

3.2 THE DATA

The data for this paper are daily closing prices for energy commodities futures. Six series are studied and the samples are as follows: crude oil from 30-3-83 to 23-1-98, electricity from 1-4-96 to 23-1-98, heating oil from 2-6-80 to 23-1-98, natural gas from 3-

4-90 to 23-1-98, propane from 21-8-87 to 23-1-98 and unleaded gas from 3-12-84 to 23-1-98.

For all six series I use the logs of the levels and since the estimation and forecasts as I will show later require the first differences of the logged series, in Table 3.1 I present the summary statistics for the first differences of the data. We can see that the null hypothesis of normality according to the Jarque-Berra statistic is rejected for all series. In Figures 3.1-3.6 I graph the logs of the six energy series. From these figures we observe that the low moments for these series do not seem to be constant over time. Specifically, the mean does not seem to be constant over time and thus I will test for the presence of stochastic trends to these data series. The variances also do not seem to be constant as we observe periods of high volatility and relative tranquility in the respective graphs. This points to the direction of ARCH/GARCH effects in the data and I will formally test in section 4 for the presence of such processes, after the identification of the most appropriate autoregressive model.

3.3 MODELING VOLATILITY IN ECONOMICS TIME SERIES

The assumption in conventional econometrics is that the variance of the error term is constant, or in other words that the disturbances are homoskedastic. However, observing the actual series we can find periods of relative tranquility and other periods where there is unusually large volatility. Thus, the assumption of homoskedasticity is not appropriate. In terms of economic forecasts, it may be very important to forecast the conditional variance of a series: for an asset holder who plans to hold the asset for some short period of time, the unconditional (or the long-run) variance is of little importance. The unconditional variance provides information about the volatility and risk of the asset over its lifetime. An estimate of the variance of the underlying asset for the investor's holding period, given past history, would be more appropriate.

3.3.1   ARCH PROCESSES

Engle (1982) using a model of the U.K. inflation shows that large and small forecast errors tend to appear in clusters. This suggests that the variance of the forecast error has a form of heteroskedasticity that depends on previous values of the error term. He called this type of heteroskedasticity *autoregressive conditional heteroskedasticity* (ARCH). This form of heteroskedasticity applies to either ARMA, ARIMA or regression models. Engle (1982) proposed the following form of an ARCH process:

$$\varepsilon_t = \nu_t \sqrt{\alpha_0 + \alpha_1 \varepsilon_{t-1}^2} \qquad (3.1.1)$$

where ν_t is a white noise process with the property that $\sigma_\nu^2 = 1$ and also that ν_t and ε_{t-1} are independent of each other and α_0, α_1 are constants such that $\alpha_0 > 0$ and $0 < \alpha_1 < 1$. Considering now the properties of the $\{\varepsilon_t\}$ sequence we can see that it has a mean of zero and its elements are not correlated. Taking the unconditional expectation of ε_t we have:

$$E\varepsilon_t = E[\nu_t (\alpha_0 + \alpha_1 \varepsilon_{t-1}^2)^{1/2}]$$

$$= Ev_t E(\alpha_0 + \alpha_1 \varepsilon_{t-1}^2)^{1/2} = 0 \qquad (3.1.2)$$

since $Ev_t = 0$. Also since $Ev_t v_{t-1} = 0$ it follows that

$$E\varepsilon_t \varepsilon_{t-1} = 0 \qquad i \neq 0. \qquad (3.1.3)$$

The unconditional variance is:

$$E\varepsilon_t^2 = E[v_t^2(\alpha_0 + \alpha_1 \varepsilon_{t-1}^2)]$$

$$= Ev_t^2 E(\alpha_0 + \alpha_1 \varepsilon_{t-1}^2)$$

$$= \alpha_0 + \alpha_1 E\varepsilon_{t-1}^2$$

and since $E\varepsilon_t^2 = E\varepsilon_{t-1}^2$, because the unconditional variance is identical, we have

$$E\varepsilon_t^2 = \alpha_0 /(1-\alpha_1). \qquad (3.1.4)$$

The above proofs show that the unconditional mean and variance of the disturbance are unaffected by the ARCH process given by equation (3.1.1). Similarly the conditional mean of ε_t is:

$$E(\varepsilon_t \mid \varepsilon_{t-1}, \varepsilon_{t-2}, \ldots) = Ev_t E(\alpha_0 + \alpha_1 \varepsilon_{t-1}^2)^{1/2} = 0. \qquad (3.1.5)$$

60

Thus, so far the introduction of the ARCH process in (3.1.1) does not seem to affect the mean, variance and the conditional mean of the error term and all autocovariances are zero. Now we consider how the ARCH process affects the conditional variance. Since $\sigma_v^2 = 1$, the variance of ε_t conditional on the past history ε_{t-1}, ε_{t-2}, ... is

$$E(\varepsilon_t^2 \mid \varepsilon_{t-1}, \varepsilon_{t-2}, ...) = \alpha_0 + \alpha_1 \varepsilon_{t-1}^2. \qquad (3.1.6)$$

In (3.1.6) we can see that the conditional variance depends on the realized and known ε_{t-1}^2. The higher the disturbance in the previous period is the higher the conditional variance will be. The conditional variance of equation (3.1.6) follows an autoregressive process which is denoted as ARCH(1). Because the conditional variance must always be positive, we have to put restrictions on the coefficients α_0 and α_1 which have to be positive. Also in order for (3.1.6) to be convergent we need that $0 < \alpha_1 < 1$.

The important features of the ARCH process are that both the conditional and the unconditional mean of the error term are zero, the unconditional variance is constant, and the errors are not serially correlated since for $s \neq 0$, $E\varepsilon_t \varepsilon_{t-s} = 0$. But the errors are not independent from each other. The ARCH process introduces a correlation of the errors through their second moments. This makes the errors conditionally heteroskedastic and the underlying time series an ARCH process as well. If the process that generates a random variable y can be described as

$$y_t = \phi_0 + \phi_1 y_{t-1} + \varepsilon_t \qquad (3.1.7)$$

then the t+1 period forecast of y will be

$$E_t y_{t+1} = \phi_0 + \phi_1 y_t . \qquad (3.1.8)$$

To explain the dynamics of this simple model, when the error term in (3.1.7) has an ARCH process as described in (3.1.1), consider an unusually high (in absolute terms) shock to v_t . This will produce a high disturbance ε_{t+1} and a high variance for the error. The higher ϕ_1 is the more y will depart from its mean, thus increasing its variance. The higher ϕ_1 is, the more persistent the deviation from the mean will be and the higher the variance of y. Specifically, the conditional mean and variance of y will be:

$$E_{t-1} y_t = \phi_0 + \phi_1 y_{t-1} \qquad (3.1.9)$$

and

$$Var(y_t \mid y_{t-1}, y_{t-2},...) = E_{t-1}(y_t - \phi_0 - \phi_1 y_{t-1})^2$$

$$= E_{t-1}(\varepsilon_t)^2$$

$$= \alpha_0 + \alpha_1 (\varepsilon_{t-1})^2 .$$

So the conditional variance of y_t has a minimum value of α_0 and it is positively related to α_1 and ε_{t-1}.

The above autoregressive process for the error term is called an ARCH process of order one, or an ARCH(1) process, since it includes only one lagged value of ε_t. Engle (1982) considers the more general case of q lags for the error term:

$$\varepsilon_t = v_t \sqrt{\alpha_0 + \sum_{j=1}^{q} \alpha_j \varepsilon_{t-j}^2} . \qquad (3.1.10)$$

In this case the error term ε_t is modeled as an autoregressive process of order q, so that all shocks from ε_{t-1} to ε_{t-q} have a direct effect on ε_t.

3.3.2 *THE GARCH MODEL*
Bollerslev (1986) extended Engle's work and allowed the conditional variance to be an ARMA process. In this case the error term is

$$\varepsilon_t = v_t \sqrt{h_t}$$

where

$$h_t = \alpha_0 + \sum_{j=1}^{q} \alpha_j \varepsilon_{t-j}^2 + \sum_{j=1}^{p} \beta_j h_{t-j}. \qquad (3.1.11)$$

Again in this case v_t is assumed white noise and since it is not correlated with past values of ε_t, the conditional and unconditional means of ε_t are still zero. The conditional variance now is given by h_t in equation (3.1.11). This is the generalized ARCH(p,q) model that is denoted GARCH(p,q). The GARCH(p,q) model allows for both moving average and autoregressive components in the conditional variance. It is clear that a GARCH(0,1) model is equivalent to the ARCH(1) model. In order for the GARCH conditional variance to be finite the characteristic roots of the distributed lag polynomials in (3.1.11) must all lie within the unit circle. If we represent the GARCH(p,q) process as

$$h_t = \alpha_0 + \alpha(L)\varepsilon_t^2 + \beta(L)h_t,$$

where

$$\alpha(L) = \alpha_1 L + \alpha_2 L^2 + \ldots + \alpha_q L^q,$$

$$\beta(L) = \beta_1 L + \beta_2 L^2 + \ldots + \beta_p L^p$$

and L is the lag operator. Then Bollerslev (1986) shows that the GARCH process is stationary if $\alpha(1) + \beta(1) < 1$. Here, $\alpha(1)$ and $\beta(1)$ are the polynomials $\alpha(L)$ and $\beta(L)$ evaluated at L=1:

$$\alpha(1) = \alpha_1 + \alpha_2 + ... + \alpha_q.$$

The more general GARCH model can help us capture the same dynamics of the variance from using a high order ARCH process. The advantage of this is that we have to impose fewer restrictions and it is easier to identify and estimate.

3.3.3   TESTING FOR ARCH AND GARCH PROCESSES

Engle (1982) proposes a test for ARCH disturbances in both autoregressive and regression models. In the case of an AR estimation, first we estimate the appropriate AR(n):

$$y_t = a_0 + a_1 y_{t-1} + a_2 y_{t-2} + ... + a_n y_{t-n} + \varepsilon_t. \quad (3.1.12)$$

Then we obtain the square of the fitted errors $\hat{\varepsilon}_t^2$. We regress these squared errors on a constant and q lagged values, so that we estimate:

$$\hat{\varepsilon}_t^2 = \alpha_0 + \alpha_1 \hat{\varepsilon}_{t-1}^1 + \alpha_2 \hat{\varepsilon}_{t-2}^2 + ... + \alpha_q \hat{\varepsilon}_{t-q}^2. \quad (3.1.13)$$

If there are no ARCH or GARCH effects then the coefficients α_1 to α_q must all be equal to zero and the explanatory power of the equation must be very low, which is translated into a low R^2. If the sample has T observations of disturbances then the statistic TR^2 will be distributed under the null of no ARCH or GARCH errors as a χ_q^2 distribution. If TR^2 is sufficiently large we will reject the null of no ARCH errors.

Specifying the appropriate conditional variance in the case of rejecting the null of no ARCH errors as

$$h_t = \alpha_0 + \sum_{j=1}^{q} \alpha_j \varepsilon_{t-j}^2, \qquad (3.1.14)$$

we then obtain the residuals of equation (3.1.14) and we regress them on a constant and h_{t-1}. Again the statistic TR^2 has a χ^2 distribution with one degree of freedom under the null of no GARCH process.

3.3.4 THE ARCH-M MODEL

Engle, Lilien, and Robins (1987) use the ARCH model to allow for the mean of a sequence to depend on its conditional variance. These models are called ARCH-M models and they are best suited for the modeling of asset returns. Engle, Lilien, and Robins use a model of excess returns described as

$$y_t = \mu_t + \varepsilon_t \qquad (3.1.15)$$

where y_t is the excess return from holding a long-term asset relative to the one period treasury bill or the risk free rate, μ_t is the risk premium that the typical risk averse investor needs in order to willingly hold the risky asset, and ε_t is the unforecastable error. In period t-1 the expected excess return on the risky asset must be equal to the risk premium so that

$$E_{t-1} y_t = \mu_t. \qquad (3.1.16)$$

66

In financial economics, the risk of an asset is measured by the variance of its returns. Engle, Lilien, and Robins, assume that the risk premium in equation (3.1.15) is an increasing function of the conditional variance of the unforecastable error ε_t. So now

$$\mu_t = \beta + \delta h_t, \qquad \delta > 0 \qquad\qquad (3.1.17)$$

where h_t is the conditional variance of ε_t that follows an ARCH(q) process of the form

$$h_t = \alpha_0 + \sum_{j=1}^{q} \alpha_j \varepsilon_{t-j}^2 . \qquad\qquad (3.1.18)$$

In this fashion the conditional mean of the y_t sequence depends on the conditional variance of the shocks h_t. If the conditional variance is constant, then the ARCH-M model has a constant risk premium.

The form of the ARCH-M model is determined similarly to the ARCH and GARCH models with the use of the Lagrange multiplier test (LM). The test statistic TR^2 for the LM test is distributed under the null of no ARCH-M effects as a χ^2 with degrees of freedom equal to the imposed restrictions.

3.3.5   THE EGARCH(p,q) MODEL

The ARCH and GARCH models are somewhat restrictive in the sense that they allow the conditional variance to be affected only by the size of past shocks and not their sign. Another problem with the models that we have seen thus far is that in the estimation of such processes we must impose additional restrictions to the unconditional variance parameters so that the unconditional variance remains always positive and finite. ARCH and GARCH models assume that the conditional variance is a function only of the magnitude of the lagged residuals and not their signs i.e. only the size and not the sign of lagged residuals determines the conditional variance. This assumption is restrictive and these models are not well suited to capture the so-called "leverage effect", first noted by Black (1976). Black noted that for equities, it is often observed that downward shocks to assets' prices are followed by higher volatilities than upward shocks of the same magnitude. Because of these concerns Nelson (1991) introduced a more general form for the unconditional variance the exponential GARCH(p,q) or EGARCH(p,q):

$$\log \sigma_t^2 = w_0 + \sum_{i=1}^{p} \beta_i \log \sigma_{t-i}^2 + \sum_{j=1}^{q} \left(\alpha_j \left| \frac{\varepsilon_{t-j}}{\sigma_{t-j}} \right| + \gamma_j \frac{\varepsilon_{t-j}}{\sigma_{t-j}} \right) \qquad (3.1.19)$$

In this setting, the conditional variance is expressed in logarithmic form so that it will always be positive and also the fourth term on the right hand side allows for the sign of the residuals to affect the conditional variance and in doing so it can capture the "leverage effect".

68

3.4 EMPIRICAL ESTIMATION

In this section I will first examine the stationarity properties of the series using the augmented Dickey-Fuller (ADF) and the Phillips-Peron (PP) tests for unit roots. Then I specify the appropriate autoregressive model for each of the six series and estimate the conditional variance as an ARCH, GARCH and EGARCH process. Then I compare these alternative models for the conditional variance and select the best model for each series that will be later used for forecasting.

3.4.1 TESTING FOR STOCHASTIC TRENDS IN THE DATA

It is important at this stage to examine the stationarity properties of the data and test for the presence of stochastic trends or unit roots. A stationary series has a constant mean and shocks to the series will not have permanent effects on the mean of the series. In this case the variable is mean reverting or stationary. In a series that has a stochastic trend or a unit root, a shock to the series at period t will have permanent effects. Such a series will have a non-stationary variance which will tend to infinity as $t \to \infty$. For forecasting purposes this series will not revert to a constant mean even in very long horizons and the width of the confidence intervals of the forecasts will increase without bound as the forecast horizon increases.

In testing for stochastic trends (unit roots) in the log levels of the original data, I use two alternative testing procedures as an attempt to deal with the fact that some of the series may not be very informative about the existence or not of a unit root. In columns 3 to 5, of panels A and B of Table 2, I present the results of augmented Dickey-Fuller (ADF) tests[1] to the levels and first differences of the data. In columns 6 to 8, I present the alternative non-parametric Phillips-Perron (PP) tests of Phillips and Perron (1988) for the existence of a unit root. The ADF tests are conducted using the following regression:

$$\Delta \log z_t = \alpha_0 + \alpha_1 t + \alpha_2 \log z_{t-1} + \sum_{i=1}^{m} \beta_i \Delta \log z_{t-i} + \varepsilon_t ,$$

(3.4.1)

where z_t is the series under consideration and m is selected large enough such that ε_t is white noise. The null hypothesis of a unit root is rejected if α_2 is negative and significantly different than zero. The critical values are not the usual t-statistics but are those given by Fuller (1976). The problem with this testing is that the order of the autoregression is not known. One way to overcome this is to use some information criterion to select the best model. However since the samples that I have in hand are quite large, I follow Said and Dickey (1984) who showed that the ADF test is asymptotically valid if the order of the autoregression is increased to $T^{1/3}$, where T is the sample size.

An alternative way to using the augmenting lags to correct for serial correlation is the Phillips-Peron testing procedure that uses non-parametric correction. The PP test involves estimating (3.4.1) with m=0 and then the statistics are transformed to correct for serial correlation in their asymptotic distribution. For the transformation formula see Phillips and Peron (1988, Table 3.1, p. 308-9). The critical values for this test are the same as in the

---

[1] See Dickey and Fuller (1981).

Dickey-Fuller tests. The Newey and West (1987) method is used to estimate the error variance from the estimated residuals as:

$$\frac{1}{N}\sum_{t=1}^{N}\varepsilon_t^2 + \frac{2}{N}\sum_{s=1}^{P}\omega(s,p)\sum_{t=s+1}^{N}\varepsilon_t\varepsilon_{t-s}, \qquad (3.4.2)$$

where p is the truncation lag parameter which is set in the estimation according to the Newey and West suggested value, and $\omega(s,p) = \dfrac{1-s}{p+1}$.

In panel A of Table 3.2, we have the results of the unit root tests. With respect to the ADF test, for the crude oil, electricity and heating oil series the null hypothesis of a unit root cannot be rejected at the 5% significance level. For the natural gas, propane and unleaded gas series the null of a unit root is rejected at the same significance level. According to the PP test, the null hypothesis of a unit root cannot be rejected for any of the six series. Thus, for three of the series I get conflicting results from the two tests with respect to the existence of a unit root. Having in mind the Nelson and Plosser (1982) argument that most macroeconomic time series have a unit root, I conclude in column 9 of panel A, that all series have a stochastic trend.

Next, I test the first differences of the log series for the presence of a unit root. The results are shown in panel B of Table 3.2. In this case, the null hypothesis of a unit root is rejected for all six series, and with both tests. I conclude that the first differences of the logs are stationary.

3.4.2   *AR MODEL SPECIFICATION*

Having concluded in the previous section that all six energy futures have a unit root, I will now use the first differences of the log series to select the best fitting autoregressive model (AR) for each of the series:

$$\Delta y_t = \phi_0 + \sum_{i=1}^{m} \phi_i \Delta y_{t-i} + \varepsilon_t, \qquad (3.4.3)$$

where y_t is the log of the series in question and m is the order of the autoregression. To select the number of AR lags in (3.4.3) for each series, I estimate (3.4.3) using m=1 and progressively increase the number of autoregressive lags until ε_t is not serially correlated. To test for autocorrelation in the residuals, I use the Ljung-Box Q-statistic. Then, I estimate several models with higher AR orders and choose the number of autoregressive lags, m, that minimizes the Akaike and Swartz information criteria, AIC and SIC respectively. Whenever the two information criteria select different orders of autoregression for a series, the fact that these models are nested, allows me to perform a likelihood ratio test (LR) to select the optimum number of lags. As an extra step, after selecting an AR(m) order according to the above, I overfit the model including additional lags and then perform both a LR and an F-test to determine whether these lags improve significantly the fit of the AR process.

Following this procedure, I find that for the crude oil, both the AIC and the SIC select an AR(10) model for which the probability of the Ljung-Box Q-statistic is 0.056. The LR-test for AR(10) against an AR(15) produces an LR statistic equal to 5.73. This is distributed under the null that AR(10) is correct, as a χ^2 with 5 degrees of freedom. The probability of 5.73 is 0.333. Also an F-test of the null that $\phi_{11} = ... = \phi_{15} = 0$ is equal to 1.14 with a probability of 0.336. So I conclude that the correct AR specification for crude oil is an AR(10).

Similarly, for electricity and unleaded gas both the AIC and SIC select an AR(4) and AR(10) model respectively, with the LR and F-statistics on overfitted models being statistically insignificant. For the heating oil the AIC selects an AR(14) while the SIC selects an AR(11). The likelihood ratio test between the two AR specifications provides a test statistic of 9.27 which has a probability of 0.02587. Thus, it is statistically significant at the 5% level. The F-test that the coefficients of the lags 12 through 14 are all equal to zero yields an F-statistic equal to 3.08 with probability 0.02623. Thus, I select the AR(14) model. For natural gas AIC and SIC select 23 and 14 lags respectively, with the LR and F-test rejecting the adequacy of the AR(14) and selecting the AR(23). Finally for propane, the AIC and the SIC select 13 and 11 lags respectively and additional tests show that the AR(13) is the appropriate model. These results are summarized in Table 3.3.

3.4.3   *ESTIMATING THE APPROPRIATE ARCH MODEL*

Having already estimated the appropriate autoregressive model for each of the six series, we now need to formally test the residuals of those autoregressive models for the presence of ARCH processes. Visually inspecting the autocorrelation and partial autocorrelation functions of the residuals of the autoregressions, we do not find any evidence of autocorrelation and the Ljung-Box Q(36) statistic is not significant for any of the series. From this we conclude that there is no linear dependence in the residuals of the autoregressions. However the $Q^2(36)$, which represents the Q-statistic for the squared residuals is highly significant. This implies that there is higher order dependence in the residuals. The Q^2-statistic is designed to pick non-linearities and the presence of conditional heteroscedasticity. Thus, now we have evidence for non-linearities in the data and conditional heteroscedasticity. I need to formally test for the presence of ARCH/GARCH processes in the residuals. Engle (1982) proposes the following Lagrange multiplier test for ARCH disturbances: I obtain the residuals from the autoregressions and I square them. Then, I regress these residuals against a constant and q lagged values of the squared residuals, so I estimate:

$$\varepsilon_t^2 = \alpha_0 + \sum_{i=1}^{q} \alpha_i \varepsilon_{t-i}^2 \, . \qquad (3.4.4)$$

If there are no ARCH or GARCH effects then the estimated coefficients α_1 through α_q should be equal to zero. Thus, this regression will have little explanatory power and the coefficient of determination R^2 will be very low. If the sample size is T, under the null hypothesis of no ARCH errors, the test statistic TR^2 converges to a χ_q^2 distribution. If TR^2 is sufficiently large, rejection of the null hypothesis that the coefficients of the lagged squared residuals are all equal to zero is equivalent to rejecting the null hypothesis of no ARCH errors. In Table 3.4, I present the results from the Lagrange multiplier tests for each series. I use one, two, five and ten lags. As it is obvious from the test statistics and the corresponding probabilities, I reject the null of no ARCH processes in the residuals for all series and all lag structures, with the exception of the electricity where the test statistic

74

appears to be insignificant at lags one and two. For higher lag orders, five and ten, we reject

the null of no ARCH errors for electricity as well. Thus, I conclude that for all six series

there exist ARCH processes in the residuals.

With the above testing methodology we can detect the existence of conditional

heteroscedasticity in the errors, but we cannot identify the specific order of the ARCH. To

find the order of the ARCH(q) that best fits the data, I estimate an ARCH(q) model for

each of the series, with q = 1,2, …,9. Then I report the AIC and SIC from each estimated

model to help for the selection of the optimal order of ARCH. This estimation is performed

using maximum likelihood estimation (ML). The advantages of the ML is that (a) it allows

for joint estimation of the mean and variance equation. (b) we can use likelihood ratio tests

of restrictions of the model. (c) consistency of the ML estimator for the parameters of the

variance does not require the existence of fourth or higher moments of the data which is

typically required for the consistence of the least squares (LS) estimator.

To identify q in the variance equation, I use the likelihood ratio test (LR). Under

the null hypothesis that q is correct, the LR test statistic:

$$LR(q) = 2[\max L(\theta_{q+1}) - \max L(\theta_q)] \qquad (3.4.5)$$

where θ_q is the parameter vector with q lags in the ARCH term, is asymptotically

distributed as a χ^2 with 1 degree of freedom. So, if the LR statistic is significant this

means that the q+1 lag specification in the ARCH is more appropriate than q, and I choose the value of q for which the LR test statistic is not significant at 1%. In Table 3.5, I present the LR test statistic. The critical value at the 1% significance level with 1 degree of freedom is 6.63.

According to this, the LR test statistic becomes insignificant at the 9th lag for crude oil, so the optimal lag length is 8. For electricity, the LR statistic becomes insignificant at the 4th lag, so we may choose 3 lags for the order of ARCH, but when we continue adding lags, the statistic becomes again significant at the 9th lag. To select between the ARCH(3) and ARCH(9) processes I perform an LR test between q=3 and q=9. The LR tests statistic is equal to 9.73 and the critical value at the 1% level with 6 degrees of freedom is 16.81. So we accept the null hypothesis that ARCH(3) is the correct specification. For heating oil, the LR statistic is significant at all lag lengths, so I conclude that the correct length of ARCH lags is greater than 9. In the natural gas, we have a case similar to electricity. The 3rd and 6th lags appear to be appropriate since the LR statistic becomes insignificant at the 4th lag but it is significant again at the 6th lag. Again I employ a LR test between ARCH(3) and ARCH(6) which produces a tests statistic of 26.58, with a critical value at the 1% level with 3 degrees of freedom of 11.34. So, I reject the null and I select the ARCH(6) as the correct specification q. For propane all lags are highly significant and I conclude that the correct lag length q is greater than 9. Finally, the unleaded gas LR test suggests both the 3rd and 6th lags for the q, and again a LR test between the two lag structures, ARCH(3) and ARCH(6), has a statistic of 83.57 with a critical value of 11.34. So, I conclude that the ARCH(6) is the most appropriate model.

I also use the value of the minimized AIC and SIC to select the best ARCH lag. When the number of observations is large, as in our samples, SIC penalizes additional parameters much more than AIC, leading to more parsimonious models. Geweke and Meese (1981) show that asymptotically SIC correctly identifies an ARMA model, while AIC tends to overfit the model. There is no proof however that the ARCH model satisfies the conditions for this result.

In Table 3.6, I summarize the order of ARCH that is selected according to the LR tests, the AIC and SIC.

3.4.4 FITTING AN APPROPRIATE GARCH MODEL

As we have seen, Bollerslev's (1986) GARCH model is a generalization of the pure ARCH model. The conditional variance is not assumed to depend only on the lagged values of squared residuals, but it is allowed to depend on lagged values of itself-an autoregressive component is introduced. In the previous section, I concluded that the appropriate lag structure for the ARCH representation of the conditional variance is relatively long with lags from 6 to greater than 9 with the exception of electricity where the best fitting model was an ARCH(3). In a GARCH(1,1) model:

$$h_t = \alpha_0 + \alpha_1 \varepsilon_{t-1}^2 + \beta_1 h_{t-1}, \qquad (3.4.6)$$

if $\beta_1 < 1$, then the GARCH(1,1) model is actually equivalent to an ARCH model with infinite lags since from (3.4.6) we have

$$h_t = \alpha_0 (1 + \beta_1 + \beta_1^2 + \ldots) + \alpha_1 (\varepsilon_{t-1}^2 + \beta_1 \varepsilon_{t-2}^2 + \beta_1^2 \varepsilon_{t-3}^2, \ldots),$$

so that we get

$$h_t = \frac{\alpha_0}{1-\beta_1} + \alpha_1 \sum_{i=0}^{\infty} \beta_1^i \varepsilon_{t-1-i}^2 . \qquad (3.4.7)$$

If we set $\alpha_1 = 1$ and use only a finite number of lags then we have an ARCH model with geometrically declining weights:

$$h_t = \zeta_0 + \sum_{i=1}^{q} \beta_1^i \varepsilon_{t-i}^2 . \qquad (3.4.8)$$

Thus, it is possible that a GARCH(1,1) representation will fit the energy data better. The added advantage of a GARCH(1,1) model is the more parsimonious representation which requires the estimation of only two additional parameters while with the ARCH models we found that many more parameters have to be estimated.

For every energy series I estimate the models GARCH(p,q) with p = 1, 2 and q = 1,2. So, four different GARCH models are estimated for every series. These models are not all nested, so I cannot use a likelihood ratio test to select the best GARCH representation. Nonetheless, since all four models belong to the general class of GARCH(p,q) models I can use the AIC, SIC or the adjusted R^2 for model selection. The problem with the adjusted R^2 criterion is that it is valid only if the correct model is within the ones tested and it will

78

select the true model only 50% of the time. Because of these restrictions, I will rely on the AIC (1974) and SIC (1978) to select the best GARCH model. In Table 3.7, I present the AIC, SIC, adjusted R^2, and the value of the maximized log-likelihood function for four different GARCH models of the six energy variables. All three criteria select the GARCH(1,1) as the best model except for natural gas where all three criteria select the GARCH(2,1) as the best fitting model.

3.4.5   FITTING AN EGARCH(1,1) MODEL

To address the restrictions of the ARCH and GARCH problems as it was discussed earlier I use Nelson's (1991) exponential GARCH(1,1) or EGARCH(1,1), also inspired by Engle's (1982) ARCH model. Now the conditional variance depends on both the size and the sign of lagged residuals and I model the conditional variance as

$$\log \sigma_t^2 = w_0 + \beta \log \sigma_{t-1}^2 + \alpha \left| \frac{\varepsilon_{t-1}}{\sigma_{t-1}} \right| + \gamma \frac{\varepsilon_{t-1}}{\sigma_{t-1}}. \tag{3.4.9}$$

The log transformation insures that σ_t^2 remains non-negative for all t. In this case the impact of the most recent residual is now exponential rather than quadratic. In Table 3.8, I present the AIC, SIC, adjusted R^2 and the maximized log-likelihood statistics from the estimation of an EGARCH(1,1) model for each of the six energy series.

3.4.6   MODEL SELECTION

Thus far, I have selected the best ARCH and GARCH specification and estimated an EGARCH(1,1) model for the six energy series. The next step is to choose which of the three different model specifications best fits the data. Comparing the ARCH and GARCH models, these models are not nested, and thus, I cannot use a likelihood ratio test to select the best model. But both ARCH(q*) and GARCH(p*,q*)[2] models belong to the larger GARCH(p,q) class, so I can use the AIC, SIC and adjusted R^2 to select between the two.

In Table 3.9, I present the AIC, SIC and the value of the maximized log-likelihood function for the ARCH(q*) and GARCH(p*,q*) models. For the cases of the heating oil and propane where the likelihood ratio test does not become insignificant even at the ninth lag, I use the statistics from the ARCH(9) model. Clearly for all six series the GARCH representation is superior to the ARCH according to both AIC and SIC. So for all series the selected model is a GARCH(1,1) with the exception of natural gas where it is GARCH(2,1). This result is somewhat expected as the long lag structures of the best fitted ARCH models imply that a GARCH(1,1) may be more appropriate as explained previously.

Having concluded that the GARCH(p*,q*) specification is superior to the ARCH(q*), the next step is to compare the GARCH(p*,q*) models with the EGARCH(1,1) that I have already estimated. The AIC and SIC in Tables 3.8 and 3.9, both select the GARCH(p*,q*) models for all energy series except for the natural gas where the EGARCH(1,1) model is selected.

I also present the diagnostics on the standardized residuals from the GARCH(p*,q*) and EGARCH(1,1) models. These are calculated as:

---

[2] Where p* and q* represent the optimal lags as they were estimated in sections 4.3 and 4.4.

$$\xi_t = \frac{\hat{\varepsilon}_t}{\sqrt{h_t}}, \qquad (3.4.10)$$

where $\hat{\varepsilon}_t$ are the residuals from the estimated model and h_t is the estimated conditional variance. If the model is correctly specified then ξ_t will have a mean of zero, variance one, and be iid. The diagnostics for the standardized residuals, mean, variance, skeweness, kurtosis and the Jarque-Berra statistic for normality, are presented in Table 3.10. The lower the Jarque-Berra statistic is, the closer the corresponding standardized residuals are to normality.

In order for the unconditional variance to exist in each of the estimated models, we need α_0, α_1, and β_1, all to be greater or equal to zero so that the unconditional variance is always positive. Also, the unconditional variance is finite if $\alpha_1 + \sum_{i=1}^{p^*} \beta_i < 1$ in the GARCH models and $\beta < 1$ in the EGARCH model. In Table 3.11, I present in panels A and B, the estimated coefficients on the conditional variance for both the GARCH(p^*,q^*) and the EGARCH(1,1) models respectively, and I test the hypotheses that $\alpha_1 + \sum_{i=1}^{p^*} \beta_i = 1$ and $\beta = 1$. It is clear from columns eight and nine on panel A, that only in the cases of the electricity and unleaded gas we can reject the null hypothesis of an infinite unconditional variance. In the other four series we cannot reject the null hypothesis that $\alpha_1 + \sum_{i=1}^{p^*} \beta_i = 1$, and thus the unconditional variance for these series will not be stationary. From column eight in panel

B, we can see that the null hypothesis of a non-stationary unconditional variance is rejected

for all series except electricity. According to these test results, only three of the previously

selected models appear adequate, and these are the GARCH(1,1) models for electricity and

unleaded gas, and the EGARCH(1,1) model for natural gas. The GARCH(1,1) models for

crude oil, heating oil, and propane produce infinite unconditional variances so that the

EGARCH(1,1) model is selected instead.

Thus, I have concluded that the best model for electricity and unleaded gas is a

GARCH(1,1) and for crude oil, heating oil, natural gas, and propane is an EGARCH(1,1).

It would be interesting at this point to see whether the inclusion of the conditional

variance in the mean equation has any effect on the mean of the series. Thus, I estimate the

corresponding GARCH(p*,q*)-M model for electricity and unleaded gas, and an

EGARCH(1,1)-M model is estimated for the rest of the series. In the second column of

Table 3.12, I present the type of model that is estimated for each of the series, the third

column presents the number of AR lags that are included in the mean equation, while in

columns three to five I report the estimated coefficient of the conditional variance, b, the

corresponding t-statistic, and the probability respectively. The coefficient of the

conditional variance, b, is not statistically significant for five out of the six series at the

conventional 5% significance level, so I conclude that the inclusion of the conditional

variance in the mean equation does not improve the fit of the model for these five series.

However, the coefficient b, for the case of propane appears to be statistically significant at

the 5% level, with a t-statistic of –2.266648 and a probability of 0.0235. Thus, the

EGARCH(1,1)-M model for propane is selected over the EGARCH(1,1).

Summarizing model selection, I have selected a GARCH(1,1) model for electricity and unleaded gas, an EGARCH(1,1) for crude oil, heating oil, and natural gas, and an EGARCH(1,1)-M for propane. In Table 3.13, I present the estimated coefficients for the conditional variances of these models and in Figures 3.7 to 3.12, I graph the conditional variances. For electricity and unleaded gas that are estimated using a GARCH(1,1) model, all coefficients of the conditional variance appear to be statistically significant. For the series that an EGARCH(1,1) model was selected, crude oil, heating oil and natural gas, all coefficients are statistically different than zero except for the parameter γ that is insignificant for all three series. The same is true for propane which is estimated using an EGARCH(1,1)-M model. All parameters are highly significant except for the last coefficient, γ, which again appears insignificant. Since the fourth term in the EGARCH and EGARCH-M models is designed to capture the effects of the sign of the lagged residuals to the asset's variance, and the coefficient of this term, γ, appears insignificant, this means that the variance of the changes in the assets' prices does not depend on the sign of the residuals. Thus, there is no leverage effect.

The estimated β s or the lagged conditional variances in the conditional variance equation for all six series although different than one as tested earlier, are very close to one. This means that the conditional variance will exhibit high persistence and the effects of the shocks will fade away very slowly.

The Box-Pierce $Q(36)$ and $Q^2(36)$ statistics show that we fail to reject the null hypotheses that there are no linear or non-linear processes in the residuals that we haven't accounted for. Only the $Q^2(36)$ statistic for natural gas is statistically significant, implying that there are still some non-linear processes in the errors that the best fitted model, an EGARCH(1,1), cannot pick-up.

3.5 FORECASTING

In the previous section I selected the best model for each of the six energy series. In this section I will use these models to produce in sample forecasts and compare the forecasted values with the actual realized futures prices. To do this I will exclude the last 22 observations from the estimation, since the data I use are daily futures closing prices, and the 22 observations represent approximately one month's trading days. Then I use the remaining observations to re-estimate the best fitted model for each series and use these models to generate in-sample forecasts for the last 22 observations. The exclusion of the last 22 observations leaves me with 3701 observations for crude oil, 434 for electricity, 4410 for heating oil, 1942 for natural gas, 2600 for propane and 3278 for unleaded gas.

In Figures 3.13-3.18 I present the graphs of the forecasts. The solid line represents the realized value, the thick dashed line represents the forecasted values, and the other two dashed lines represent the ± 2 standard deviations confidence bands for the forecasts. These standard deviations are estimated from the forecasted conditional variances. In Table 3.14 I present some statistics for the forecasts' evaluation. These statistics are: the root mean squared error (RMSE),

$$RMSE = \sqrt{\frac{1}{T}\sum_{t=1}^{T} e_{t+1,t}^{2}}, \qquad (3.5.1)$$

84

where $e_{t+1,t} = y_{t+1} - y_{t+1,t}$, and y_{t+1} is the actual value of variable y at period t+1 and $y_{t+1,t}$ is the forecast for y_{t+1} at period t. The mean absolute error (MAE) is defined as:

$$MAE = \frac{1}{T}\sum_{t=1}^{T}\left|e_{t+1,t}\right|, \qquad (3.5.2)$$

and the mean absolute percent error is:

$$MAPE = \frac{1}{T}\sum_{t=1}^{T}\left|p_{t+1,t}\right| \qquad (3.5.3)$$

where $p_{t+1,t} = (y_{t+1} - y_{t+1,t})/y_{t+1}$. Finally Theil's inequality coefficient is defined as:

$$U = \frac{\sqrt{\frac{1}{T}\sum_{t=1}^{T}(y_{t+1} - y_{t+1,t})^2}}{\sqrt{\frac{1}{T}\sum_{t=1}^{T}y_{t+1}^2} + \sqrt{\frac{1}{T}\sum_{t=1}^{T}y_{t+1,t}^2}}. \qquad (3.5.4)$$

As we can see from Figures 3.13-3.18, the actual value of the closing price for the six futures contracts falls within the ± 2 conditional standard deviations band of the forecast for all forecasted values except for observation 3710 for crude oil and observation 4419 for heating oil where in both cases the realized closing price was below the predicted

85

confidence band. Thus, the model appears to be able to predict well in the short forecasting horizon of 22 periods in the future or approximately one month.

The most important result from modeling and estimating the conditional heteroscedasticity for forecasting is that conditional forecasts are far more superior than unconditional forecasts. This is because the forecast error using the conditional forecasts is smaller than the error from unconditional forecasts. To see this improvement in the forecasts in Table 3.15 I present the unconditional forecast standard deviations for the six series in columns 3 and 7, and in columns 4 and 8 the conditional standard deviation for one to five days ahead forecasts. In these one week ahead forecasts the unconditional standard deviation is always greater than the conditional one and we can verify the theoretical superiority of the conditional forecasts. Thus, using the conditional heteroscedasticity to model the error sequence we are able to construct narrower forecasting confidence bands. Using such models, an investor optimizing his portfolio can use a more precise measure of risk for the corresponding assets.

3.6 CONCLUSIONS

In this paper I tried to model the time series behavior of six energy market variables, the closing futures prices for crude oil, electricity, heating oil, natural gas, propane, and unleaded gas. Testing these series with two different unit root tests-the ADF and the Phillips-Peron-I showed that all six series have a stochastic trend. The non-stationarity of the series in their logarithmic forms suggested the use of their first differences as the appropriate variables for the rest of the analysis. I modeled the data as an AR(p) process where the order of the autoregression, p, was selected in such a way as to remove serial correlation. Having accounted for any linear dependencies in the data I proceeded to test for non-linear processes in the errors. The clustering of volatility episodes that was observed in the data implied a non-constant conditional variance and the existence of a time-varying heteroskedasticity. The application of more formal tests to the residuals confirmed the existence of ARCH processes in the errors. Different models of conditional heteroskedasticity that have been proposed recently in the literature were applied and tested and I selected for each series the model that provided the best fit. These best fitted models were then used to produce in-sample forecasts for one month ahead. Confidence bands were also constructed based on the forecasted conditional variance of the series. The actual values of the six energy market futures series were within the predicted +/-2 standard deviations bands for all forecasted values but two. Finally, using the conditional heteroscedasticity we saw that we can provide forecasts with smaller forecast errors than with the usual unconditional forecasts, verifying the theoretical superiority of such forecasts.

TABLE 3.1

SUMMARY STATISTICS FOR DAILY ENERGY PRICES (FIRST DIFFEREMCES IN LOGS)

Variable	Sample Size	Mean	Standard. Dev.	Min	Max	Skewness	Kurtosis	J-B Prob.*
Crude Oil	3722	-0,000163	0,019	-0,384071	0,123525	-2,106	47,409	0,000
Electricity	455	0,000955	0,043	-0,297022	0,267433	-1,105	18,680	0,000
Heating Oil	4431	-0,000133	0,019	-0,350938	0,128019	-1,907	36,303	0,000
Natural Gas	1962	0,000129	0,028	-0,230920	0,209216	-0,121	13,864	0,000
Propane	2621	0,000003	0,021	-0,378558	0,113597	-3,334	57,593	0,000
Unleaded Gas	3299	-0,000116	0,019	-0,298099	0,147865	-1,060	23,400	0,000

* The null hypothesis is that the series is normally distributed.

TABLE 3.2

UNIT ROOT TEST RESULTS IN THE ENERGY VARIABLES

Panel A. Tests on the log levels

Variable	Sample Size	Augmented Dickey-Fuller Tests			Phillips-Peron Tests			Decision
		ADF Statistic	Aug. Lags	5% Crit. Value	PP Statistic	Tranc. Lags	5% Crit. Value	
Crude Oil	3723	-2,95	16	-3,41	-2,77	8	-3,41	I(1)
Electricity	456	-1,87	8	-3,42	-2,04	5	-3,42	I(1)
Heating Oil	4432	-3,15	16	-3,41	-2,85	9	-3,41	I(1)
Natural Gas	1963	-3,65	13	-3,42	-3,20	7	-3,42	I(1)
Propane	2622	-4,04	14	-3,42	-3,17	8	-3,41	I(1)
Unleaded Gas	3300	-3,44	15	-3,41	-3,36	8	-3,41	I(1)

Panel B. First differeneces of log levels

Variable	Sample Size	Augmented Dickey-Fuller Tests			Phillips-Peron Tests			Decision
		ADF Statistic	Aug. Lags	5% Crit. Value	PP Statistic	Tranc. Lags	5% Crit. Value	
Crude Oil	3723	-13,68	16	-3,41	-59,16	8	-3,41	I(0)
Electric Power	456	-7,69	8	-3,42	-20,78	5	-3,42	I(0)
Heating Oil	4432	-14,91	16	-3,41	-63,83	9	-3,41	I(0)
Natural Gas	1963	-10,18	13	-3,42	-42,02	7	-3,42	I(0)
Propane	2622	-11,19	14	-3,41	-42,58	8	-3,41	I(0)
Unleaded Gas	3300	-13,92	15	-3,41	-53,57	8	-3,41	I(0)

TABLE 3.3

SELECTION OF THE APPROPRIATE AR LAG STRUCTURE

Variable	AIC lag Selection	Value of min AIC	SIC lag Selection	Value of min SIC	LR Test Statistic	Prob.	F-Test Statistic	Prob.	Optimal AR lag structure	Box-Pierce Q(36) statistic
Crude Oil	10	-7,890061	10	-7,87163	5.731*	0,333	1.142*	0,336	10	0,056
Electricity	4	-6,296094	4	-6,25051	7.942*	0,242	1.303*	0,255	4	0,270
Heating Oil	14	-7,993264	11	-7,97584	9,273	0,026	3,084	0,026	14	0,751
Natural Gas	23	-7,158198	14	-7,11074	35,700	0,000	3,954	0,000	23	1,000
Propane	13	-7,788038	11	-7,75791	12,688	0,002	6,286	0,002	13	0,883
Unleaded Gas	10	-7,905428	10	-7,88503	2.385*	0,794	0.475*	0,795	10	0,256

* These tests involve overfitting the model selected by AIC and SIC and test the null hypothesis that the additional lags do not improve the fit.

TABLE 3.4

LAGRANGE MULTIPLIER TESTS FOR THE EXISTENCE OF ARCH ERRORS

$$\varepsilon_t^2 = \alpha_0 + \sum_{i=1}^{q} \alpha_i \varepsilon_{t-i}^2$$

Variable	Lags q	TR^2	Probability	Variable	Lags q	TR^2	Probability
Crude Oil	1	29,551	0,000	Natural Gas	1	10,008	0,002
	2	40,503	0,000		2	19,022	0,000
	5	103,492	0,000		5	22,237	0,001
	10	129,781	0,000		10	42,579	0,000
Electricity	1	1,864	0.173*	Propane	1	15,667	0,000
	2	2,038	0.361*		2	38,919	0,000
	5	21,376	0,001		5	67,156	0,000
	10	22,919	0,011		10	106,194	0,000
Heating Oil	1	16,980	0,000	Unleaded Gas	1	30,001	0,000
	2	36,713	0,000		2	55,447	0,000
	5	152,802	0,000		5	114,478	0,000
	10	195,868	0,000		10	149,314	0,000

* Not significant at the 5% level.

TABLE 3.5

LR TESTS ON ARCH MODELS

$$\Delta y_t = \varphi_0 + \sum_{j=1}^{k} \varphi_j \Delta y_{t-j} + \varepsilon_t, \varepsilon_t \mid I_{t-1} \sim N(0, h_t), h_t = \alpha_0 + \sum_{j=1}^{q} \alpha_j \varepsilon_{t-j}^2$$

ARCH Lags (q)	Crude Oil	Electricity	Heating Oil	Natural Gas	Propane	Unleaded Gas
			Likelihhod Ratio Test Statistic*			
1	.	.	.	.	.	.
2	272,47	N/A	188,66	62,35	244,69	91,06
3	307,98	40,17	174,60	7,68	205,33	71,53
4	154,78	N/A	119,90	0,12	65,30	4,10
5	94,76	3,44	55,94	6,61	68,63	61,80
6	37,82	2,98	18,90	19,83	96,10	17,66
7	56,02	1,79	32,18	2,00	17,27	4,43
8	27,30	N/A	25,60	4,51	33,68	4,62
9	1,12	11,88	53,26	3,54	10,22	0,56

* The critical value at the 1% level with 1 degree of freedom is 6.63. N/A the statistic is not available because it was not possible to achieve convergence

TABLE 3.6

ARCH MODEL SELECTION

Criterion	Crude Oil	Electricity	Heating Oil	Natural Gas	Propane	Unleaded Gas
LR Test	8	3	>9	6	>9	6
AIC	2	1	2	8	3	1
SIC	1	1	1	2	3	1

TABLE 3.7

SELECTION OF A GARCH(p,q) MODEL

$$\Delta y_t = \varphi_0 + \sum_{j=1}^{k} \varphi_j \Delta y_{t-j} + \varepsilon_t, \varepsilon_t \mid I_{t-1} \sim N(0, h_t), h_t = \alpha_0 + \alpha_1 \varepsilon_{t-1}^2 + \beta_1 h_{t-1}$$

CRUDE OIL

	AIC	SIC	Adj. R^2	Log L
GARCH(1,1)	-7.881789*	-7.858332*	0.00533*	10365,72
GARCH(1,2)	-7,881187	-7,856055	0,004998	10366,25
GARCH(2,1)	-7,880899	-7,855767	0,004712	10365,20
GARCH(2,2)	-7,880193	-7,853386	0,004276	10365,33

ELECTRICITY

	AIC	SIC	Adj. R^2	Log L
GARCH(1,1)	-6.279071*	-6.20614*	0.01821*	813,24
GARCH(1,2)	-6,266912	-6,184865	0,008359	817,43
GARCH(2,1)	-6,274653	-6,192606	0,016006	811,35
GARCH(2,2)	-6,270259	-6,179096	0,013814	813,55

HEATING OIL

	AIC	SIC	Adj. R^2	Log L
GARCH(1,1)	-7.983569*	-7.957515*	0.011502*	12170,69
GARCH(1,2)	-7,982676	-7,955176	0,010842	12172,38
GARCH(2,1)	-7,983272	-7,955771	0,011432	12168,38
GARCH(2,2)	-7,981434	-7,952486	0,009836	12170,22

TABLE 3.7 (CONTINUED)

SELECTION OF A GARCH(p,q) MODEL

NATURAL GAS

	AIC	SIC	Adj. R^2	Log L
GARCH(1,1)	-7,120578	-7,043018	-0,016461	4315,93
GARCH(1,2)	-7,136701	-7,056269	0,000305	4350,53
GARCH(2,1)	-7.139357*	-7.058925*	0.002957*	4347,11
GARCH(2,2)	-7,125997	-7,042692	-0,00994	4346,70

PROPANE

	AIC	SIC	Adj. R^2	Log L
GARCH(1,1)	-7.748555*	-7.710316*	0.038354*	7458,71
GARCH(1,2)	-7,747228	-7,70674	0,037444	7459,76
GARCH(2,1)	-7,745172	-7,704683	0,035462	7459,82
GARCH(2,2)	-7,744157	-7,701419	0,03485	7460,08

UNLEADED GAS

	AIC	SIC	Adj. R^2	Log L
GARCH(1,1)	-7.899914*	-7.873955*	0.009027*	8719,59
GARCH(1,2)	-7,899014	-7,871202	0,008435	8720,41
GARCH(2,1)	-7,899218	-7,871405	0,008637	8718,38
GARCH(2,2)	-7,898503	-7,868836	0,008228	8716,06

* These values select the corresponding GARCH model.

TABLE 3.8

EGARCH(1,1) ESTIMATION RESULTS

$$\Delta y_t = \varphi_0 + \sum_{j=1}^{k} \varphi_j \Delta y_{t-j} + \varepsilon_t, \varepsilon_t \mid I_{t-1} \sim N(0, h_t), \log h_t = w_0 + \beta \log h_{t-1} + \alpha \left| \frac{\varepsilon_{t-1}}{\sqrt{h_{t-1}}} \right| + \gamma \frac{\varepsilon_{t-1}}{\sqrt{h_{t-1}}}$$

Variable	AR Lags	AIC	SIC	Adj. R^2	Log L
Crude Oil	10	-7,881207	-7,856075	0,005018	10379,48
Electricity	4	-6,256332	-6,174285	-0,002188	829,12
Heating Oil	14	-7,983285	-7,955784	0,011444	12178,42
Natural Gas	23	-7,141221	-7,060788	0,004813	4376,44
Propane	13	-7,742823	-7,702334	0,033194	7467,93
Unleaded Gas	10	-7,898934	-7,871122	0,008356	8729,82

TABLE 3.9

SELECTION BETWEEN ARCH AND GARCH MODELS

Variable	AR Lags	ARCH(q*) Model Statistics			GARCH(p*,q*) Model Statistics			Selected Model
		AIC	SIC	Log L	AIC	SIC	Log L	
Crude Oil	10	-7,876614	-7,843105	10302,86	-7,881789	-7,858332	10365,72	GARCH(1,1)
Electricity	4	-6,269491	-6,187444	814,19	-6,279071	-6,206140	813,24	GARCH(1,1)
Heating Oil	14	-7,980340	-7,944155	12094,92	-7,983569	-7,957515	12170,69	GARCH(1,1)
Natural Gas	23	-7,119062	-7,030012	4326,14	-7,139357	-7,058925	4347,11	GARCH(2,1)
Propane	13	-7,729930	-7,675946	7449,92	-7,748555	-7,710316	7458,71	GARCH(1,1)
Unleaded Gas	10	-7,895255	-7,861880	8693,41	-7,899914	-7,873955	8719,59	GARCH(1,1)

TABLE 3.10

DIAGNOSTICS FOR THE STANDARDIZED RESIDUALS

	Crude Oil		Electricity		Heating Oil	
	GARCH	EGARCH	GARCH	EGARCH	GARCH	EGARCH
Mean	-0,0094	-0,0038	-0,0234	0,0460	-0,0114	-0,0143
Maximum	5,0233	4,6039	5,5839	7,5145	6,0003	5,7813
Mimimum	-7,2476	-8,4565	-7,4431	-5,1797	-6,4480	-7,3329
St.Deviation	0,9998	0,9999	1,0623	1,0059	0,9999	1,0000
Skewness	-0,2267	-0,2531	-1,0274	0,2462	-0,2241	-0,2577
Kurtosis	5,1469	5,6720	14,7192	16,5143	5,2640	5,5161
J-B	744,657	1143,902	2660,179	3436,584	980,303	1214,010
Prob.	0,000	0,000	0,000	0,000	0,000	0,000
Observations	3712	3712	451	451	4417	4417

	Natural Gas		Propane		Unleaded Gas	
	GARCH	EGARCH	GARCH	EGARCH	GARCH	EGARCH
Mean	-0,0296	-0,0141	-0,0016	-0,0194	0,0041	0,0020
Maximum	8,0347	7,9754	4,1877	3,9657	7,6249	7,3023
Mimimum	-9,5053	-7,9805	-9,0128	-8,1872	-6,3123	-7,0083
St.Deviation	0,9994	0,9996	1,0001	1,0006	1,0000	0,9997
Skewness	0,1165	0,4144	-0,6607	-0,6502	-0,2137	-0,2797
Kurtosis	14,1987	13,3137	8,1516	7,6465	6,0113	6,1758
J-B	10136,530	8649,484	3073,656	2529,885	1267,761	1425,062
Prob.	0,000	0,000	0,000	0,000	0,000	0,000
Observations	1939	1939	2608	2608	3289	3289

TABLE 3.11

GARCH AND EGARCH COEFFICIENTS TESTS

Panel A. GARCH(p*,q*) Model

Variable	AR Lags	(p*,q*)	Coefficients for the Conditional Variance				Test (prob.)	
			α_0	α_1	β_1	β_2	$\alpha_1+\beta_1=1$	$\alpha_1+\beta_1+\beta_2=1$
Crude Oil	10	(1,1)	0,000	0,093	0,911	-	0,350	-
Electricity	4	(1,1)	0,000	-0,014	1,001	-	0.015*	-
Heating Oil	14	(1,1)	0,000	0,082	0,915	-	0,364	-
Natural Gas	23	(2,1)	0,000	0,176	0,053	0,777	-	0,707
Propane	13	(1,1)	0,000	0,155	0,851	-	0,694	-
Unleaded Gas	10	(1,1)	0,000	0,069	0,917	-	0.041*	-

Panel B. EGARCH(1,1) Model

Variable	AR Lags	Coefficients for the Conditional Variance				Test (prob.)
		w_0	β	α	γ	$\beta=1$
Crude Oil	10	-0,184	0,993	0,162	-0,016	0.013*
Electric Power	4	-0,123	0,981	-0,004	0,142	0,422
Heating Oil	14	-0,253	0,986	0,178	0,004	0.001*
Natural Gas	23	-0,406	0,967	0,232	-0,025	0.010*
Propane	13	-0,338	0,983	0,271	0,045	0.024*
Unleaded Gas	10	-0,245	0,984	0,147	-0,003	0.002*

* Statistically significant at the 5% level.

TABLE 3.12

TESTING GARCH-M AND EGARCH-M MODELS

$$\Delta y_t = \varphi_0 + bh_t + \sum_{j=1}^{k} \varphi_j \Delta y_{t-j} + \varepsilon_t, \varepsilon_t \mid I_{t-1} \sim N(0, h_t)$$

Variable	Estimated Model	AR Lags k	Coefficient b	t-statistic	Probability
Crude Oil	EGARCH-M	10	-0,098486	-0,096007	0,9235
Electricity *	GARCH-M	4	-0,305768	-0,877635	0,3806
Heating Oil	EGARCH-M	14	-2,333717	-1,740436	0,0819
Natural Gas	EGARCH-M	23	0,268995	0,244248	0,8071
Propane	EGARCH-M	13	-2,920799	-2,266648	0,0235
Unleaded Gas	GARCH-M	10	1,615091	0,901249	0,3675

* Instead of the conditional variance the conditional standard deviation is used here.

TABLE 3.13

ESTIMATION RESULTS

Panel A. GARCH(1,1) Models

Coefficients for the Conditional Variance

Variable	AR(p)	α_0	α_1	β_1	$\square$	Log L	AIC	SIC	Q(36)	$Q^2(36)$
Electricity	4	0.000 (2.67)	-0.014 (1.47)	1.001 (156.04)		813,2434	-6,279071	-6,20614	0,341	0,51
Unleaded Gas	10	0.000 (3.27)	0.069 (4.26)	0.917 (57.14)		8719,588	-7,899914	-7,873955	0,372	0,60

Panel B. EGARCH(1,1) Models

Coefficients for the Conditional Variance

Variable	AR(p)	w_0	β	α	γ	Log L	AIC	SIC	Q(36)	$Q^2(36)$
Crude Oil	10	-0.184 (7.42)	0.993 (332.38)	0.162 (7.47)	-0.016 (1.10)	10379,48	-7,881207	-7,856075	0,213	0,45
Heating Oil	14	-0.253 (5.37)	0.986 (229.18)	0.178 (5.44)	0.004 (0.20)	12178,42	-7,983285	-7,955784	0,822	0,08
Natural Gas	23	-0.406 (3.18)	0.967 (75.25)	0.232 (3.98)	-0.025 (0.65)	4376,442	-7,141221	-7,060788	0,333	0,00

Panel C. EGARCH(1,1)-M Model

Coefficients for the Conditional Variance

Variable	AR(p)	w_0	β	α	γ	Log L	AIC	SIC	Q(36)	$Q^2(36)$
Propane	13	-0.346 (5.52)	0.982 (146.37)	0.272 (9.53)	0.040 (1.68)	7462,029	-7,745033	-7,702295	0,821	0,95

TABLE 3.14

FORECAST EVALUATION STATISTICS

Variable	Model Used for the Forecast	Forecasted Observations	RMSE	MAE	MAPE	Theil's Inequality Coef.
Crude Oil	EGARCH(1,1)	3702-3723	0,012	0,009	87,696	0,962
Electricity	GARCH(1,1)	435-456	0,022	0,020	125,203	0,900
Heating Oil	EGARCH(1,1)	4411-4432	0,013	0,010	101,458	0,978
Natural Gas	EGARCH(1,1)	1942-1963	0,025	0,021	100,872	0,765
Propane	EGARCH(1,1)-M	2601-2622	0,018	0,013	90,956	0,934
Unleaded Gas	GARCH(1,1)	3279-3300	0,012	0,010	96,679	0,948

TABLE 3.15

UNCONDITIONAL AND CONDITIONAL STANDARD DEVIATIONS IN WEEK AHEAD FORECASTS

Variable	Forecast Day	Forecast σ	$\sqrt{h_t}$	Variable	Lags q	Forecast σ	$\sqrt{h_t}$
Crude Oil	1	0,014189	0,014174	Natural Gas	1	0,032508	0,032078
	2	0,014256	0,014235		2	0,032647	0,032226
	3	0,014319	0,014295		3	0,033149	0,032370
	4	0,014382	0,014356		4	0,032854	0,032510
	5	0,014448	0,014416		5	0,033086	0,032646
Electricity	1	0,048451	0,048416	Propane	1	0,020552	0,020514
	2	0,048473	0,048414		2	0,020779	0,020565
	3	0,048463	0,048412		3	0,020836	0,020615
	4	0,048612	0,048410		4	0,020912	0,020665
	5	0,049110	0,048408		5	0,020952	0,020713
Heating Oil	1	0,012351	0,012335	Unleaded Gas	1	0,015196	0,015162
	2	0,012444	0,012423		2	0,015299	0,015235
	3	0,012531	0,012510		3	0,015367	0,015307
	4	0,012629	0,012596		4	0,015443	0,015377
	5	0,012716	0,012682		5	0,015509	0,015446

Figure 3.1. Logged Prices for Crude Oil

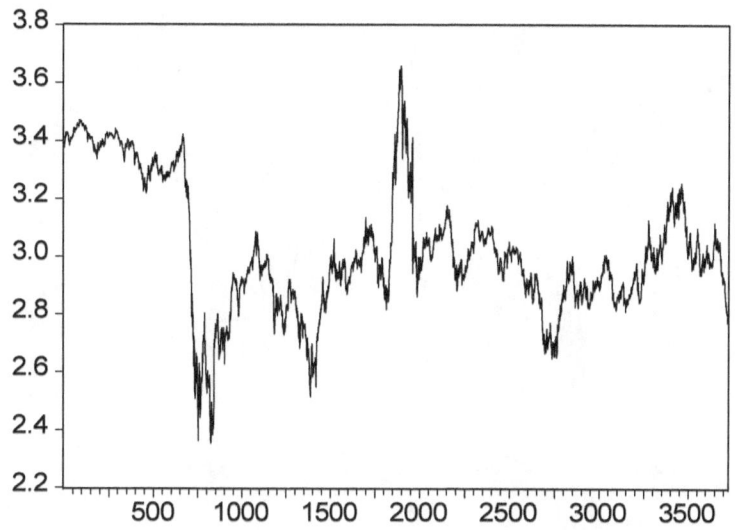

Figure 3.2. Logged Prices for Electricity

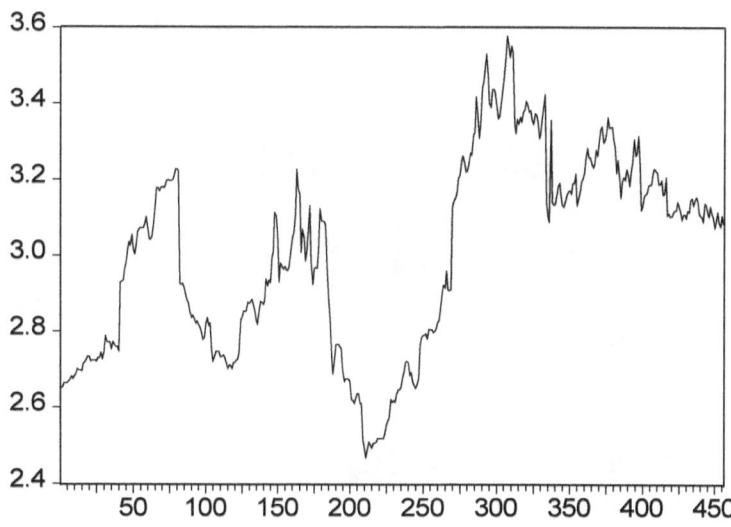

Figure 3.3. Logged Prices for Heating Oil

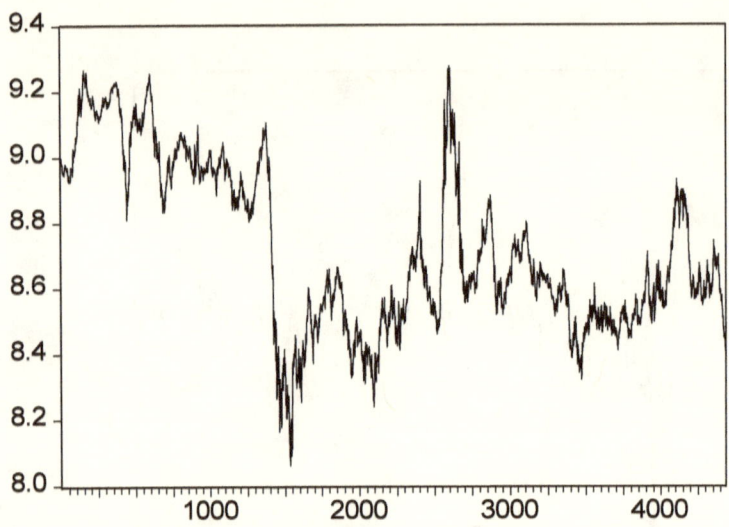

Figure 3.4. Logged Prices for Natural Gas

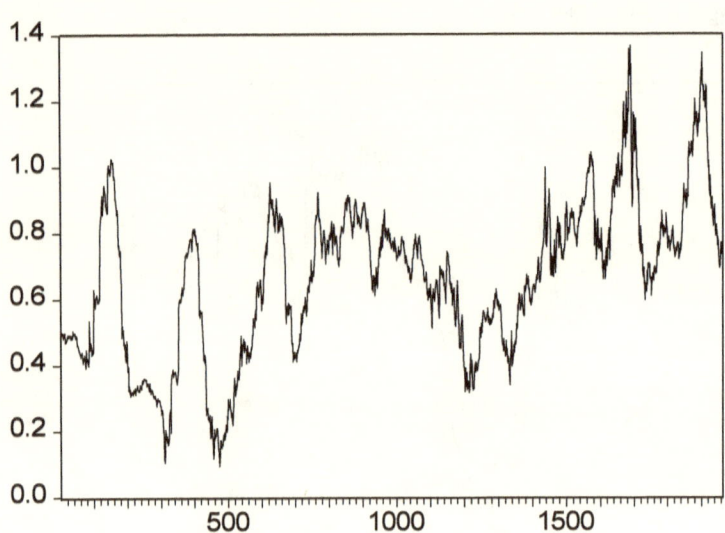

Figure 3.5. Logged Prices for Propane

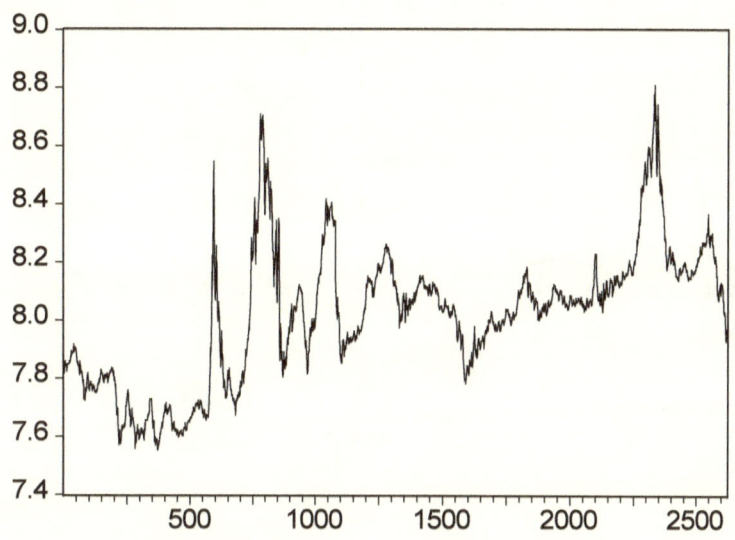

Figure 3.6. Logged Prices for Unleaded Gas

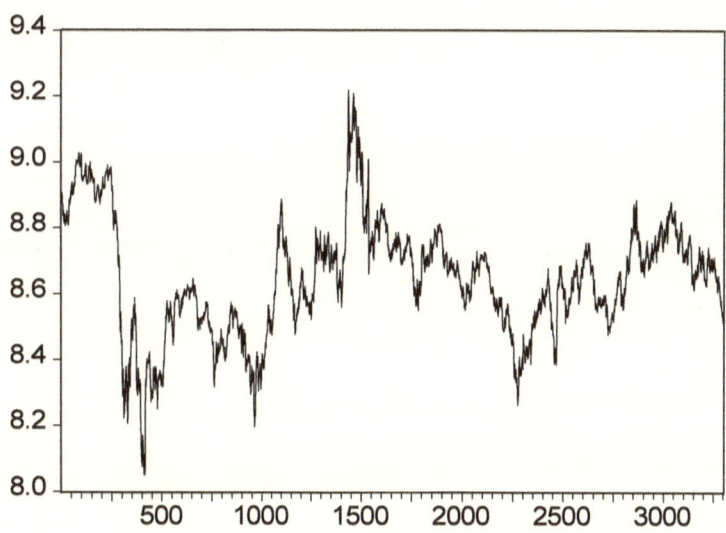

Figure 3.7. Conditional Variance for Crude Oil

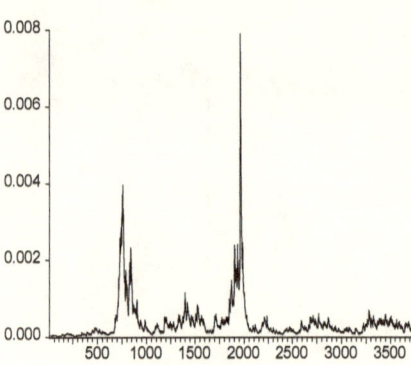

Figure 3.8. Conditional Variance for Electricity

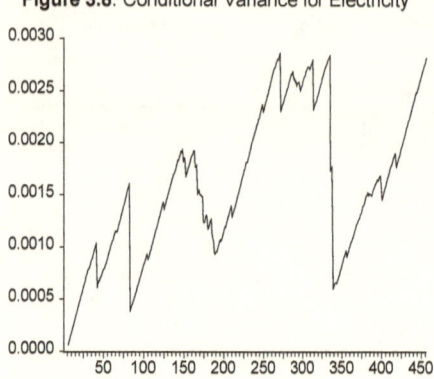

Figure 3.9. Conditional Variance for Heating Oil

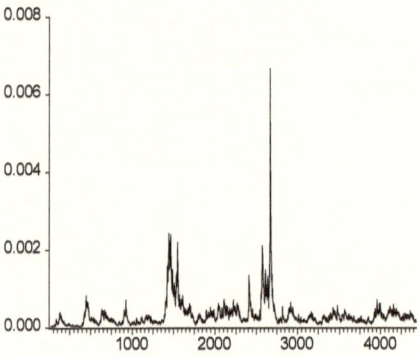

Figure 3.10. Conditional Variance for Natural Gas

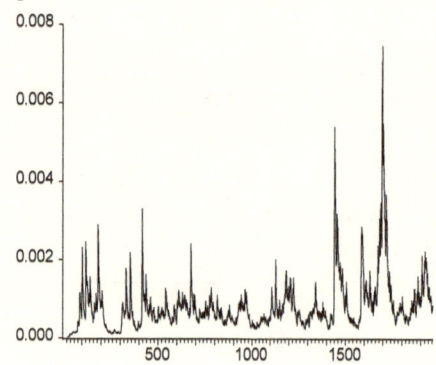

Figure 3.11. Conditional Variance for Propane

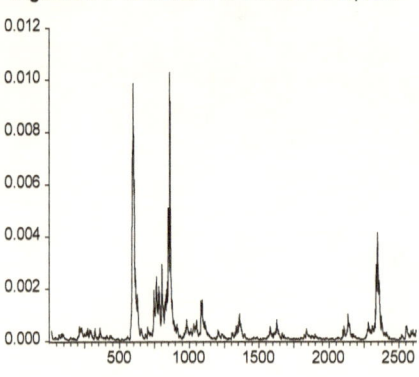

Figure 3.12. Conditional Variance for Unleaded Gas

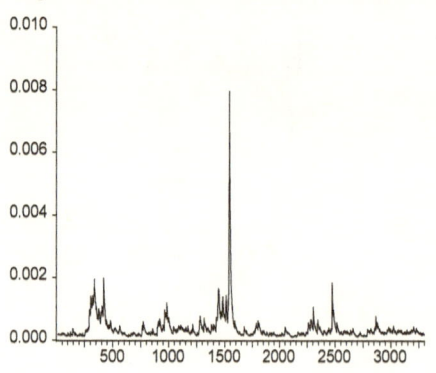

Figure 3.13. In-Sample Forecasts and 95% Confidence Intervals for Crude Oil.

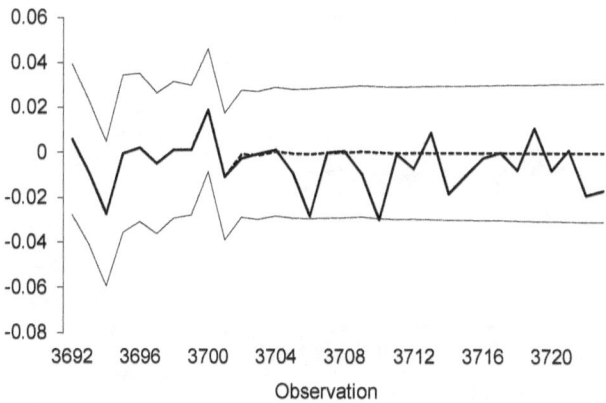

Figure 3.14. In-Sample Forecasts and 95% Confidence Intervals for Electricity.

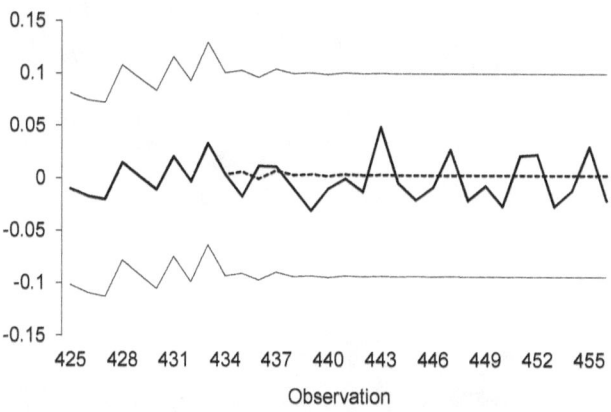

Figure 3.15. In-Sample Forecasts and 95% Confidence Intervals for Heating Oil.

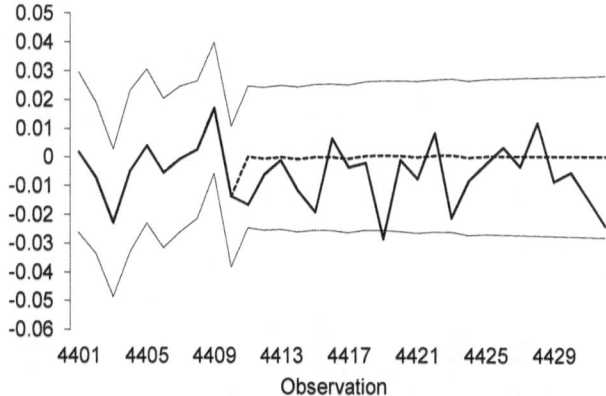

Figure 3.16. In-Sample Forecasts and 95% Confidence Intervals for Natural Gas.

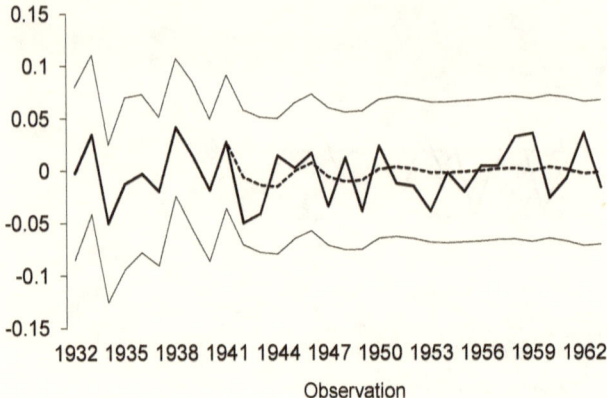

Figure 3.17. In-Sample Forecasts and 95% Confidence Intervals for Propane

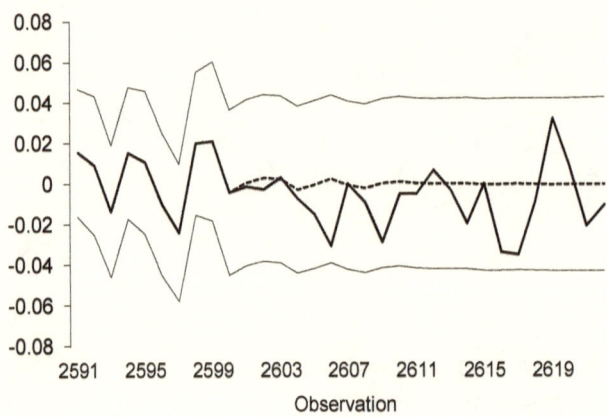

Figure 3.18. In-Sample Forecasts and 95% Confidence Intervals for Unleaded Gas.

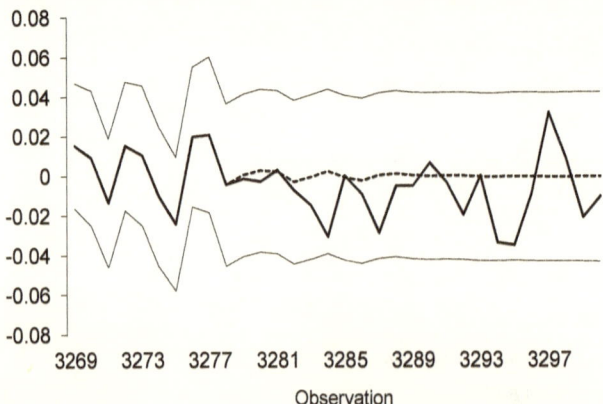

CHAPTER 4

BALANCED GROWTH, MONEY DEMAND, AND MONETARY

AGGREGATES: A COINTEGRATION APPROACH

4.1 INTRODUCTION

In development economics, the balanced growth theory suggests that in the steady state per capita consumption, investment and output all grow at the same rate so that the consumption – output and the investment – output ratios are constant. These two ratios are also known as *the great ratios*. Thus, according to the theory, consumption, investment and output must be non-stationary and for the great ratios to be constant, they must be cointegrated.

In their (1988) paper, King et al. have used a simple real business cycle model proposed by Fynn Kydland and Edward Prescott (1982) to test the balanced growth theory where total factor productivity evolves according to a random walk with drift procedure. Following King et al. (1988), in this paper we use recent developments in econometrics to test the balanced growth theory and at the same time the existence of a stable money demand function. The data that are used are quarterly U.S. observations from 1960:1 to 1997:4 for real per capita personal consumption expenditures, real per capita private fixed investment, real per capita private GNP, 3-month treasury bill interest rates and per capita real money balances. To examine the sensitivity of the results to different money measures and overcome William Barnett's (…………..) critique on the appropriate money measures I use in this paper twelve different money measures: the commonly used simple-sum M1, M2, M3 and L measures and also Divisia M1, M2, M3, and L, and currency-equivalence M1, M2, M3 and L.

The recent Johansen and Juselius (1992) multivariate maximum likelihood cointegration tests are applied to three different systems, the first including only the real variables, the second includes the nominal variables and the third all five variables. For the systems that there is evidence of the existence of cointegrated vectors according to what the theory predicts I estimate those vectors and impose additional assumptions. Finally, I simulate shocks to the whole system and to specific variables of interest and get the impulse responses of the estimated cointegrating vectors and of individual variables.

The structure of this paper is as follows: in Section 4.2, I discuss the theoretical background and show how the theory will be tested, in Section 4.3, I present the data that are used and the methods for testing for stochastic trends in the data. Section 4.4 deals with the econometric framework of the Johansen and Juselius (1992) maximum likelihood cointegration test and it's application to the three systems. In Section 4.5, the cointegrating relations that are identified in the previous section are shocked in order to see how the cointegrated vectors and individual variables respond to various stochastic shocks to the system's variables. Finally, Section 4.6, summarizes the conclusions.

4.2 THEORETICAL BACKGROUND

The model that underlies the analysis in this paper is a simple real business cycle model where we have permanent productivity shocks. It is of the general class of models described by Fynn Kydland and Edward Prescott (1982) and King et al. (1988). The economy's production function is described by a constant returns to scale Cobb-Douglas production function of the form:

$$Y_t = \lambda_t K_t^{1-\theta} N_t^{\theta} \qquad (4.2.1)$$

where Y_t is the output at period t, K_t is the capital stock and N_t represents labor. In this model it is assumed that total factor productivity λ_t follows a logarithmic random walk of the form:

$$\log(\lambda_t) = \mu_\lambda + \log(\lambda_{t-1}) + \xi_t \qquad (4.2.2)$$

112

where the innovations represented by the sequence $\{\xi_t\}$ are assumed independently and identically distributed with a mean of 0 and a variance σ^2. The interpretation of the evolution of productivity according to (4.2.2) is that the productivity grows at every period by an average rate of μ_λ and the $\{\xi_t\}$ sequence represents shocks or deviations of productivity from this average. Thus, the first two terms on the right-hand-side of (4.2.2) represent the deterministic part of the productivity evolution and the last term represents the stochastic innovations.

In a standard neoclassical model as that by Solow (1970), where we only have deterministic trends, we find that in the steady state, per capita consumption, investment and output all grow at a constant rate of μ_λ / θ. This common deterministic trend implies that the great ratios, the ratio of consumption over output and investment over output are constant in every period in the steady state. But when we add the stochastic term in the evolution of productivity, the realizations of ξ_t will permanently affect the evolution of productivity at all future periods:

$$E_t \log(\lambda_{t+s}) = E_{t-1}(\lambda_{t+s}) + \xi_t. \qquad (4.2.3)$$

In this setting, a positive productivity shock at period t raises the expected long-run growth path, introducing a common stochastic trend in the logarithms of consumption, investment and output. The stochastic trend is $\log(\lambda_t)/\theta$ and its growth rate is $(\mu_\lambda + \xi_t)/\theta$ which is the analog of the deterministic model's common growth rate μ_λ / θ. Because all three variables here, consumption, investment and output have a common stochastic trend the great ratios C_t / Y_t and I_t / Y_t must be stationary stochastic processes.

These theoretical results can be tested in a cointegration framework where $\mathbf{X}_t$ is a vector of the logarithms of consumption, investment and output at period t, denoted by c_t, i_t and y_t. All three variables are non-stationary and integrated of order 1, or I(1), because productivity as we have seen follows a random walk. The balanced growth hypothesis in this case implies that the difference between any two of the components of $\mathbf{X}_t$ will be a stationary variable or I(0) according to the Engle and Granger (1987) terminology. The two cointegrating vectors will be $\alpha =[1,0,-1]$ and $\beta =[0,1,-1]$.

In this model, the dynamic adjustments that the economy has to make after a productivity shock ξ_t and the speed of adjustment will depend on the specific characteristics and parameters of this economy regarding tastes, preferences and technology. The real business cycle theory has studied the changes that happen to the economy in terms of a) the investment technology, with respect to the issues of adjustment costs, inventory changes and time-to-build, b) the production technology, with respect to variable capacity utilization, indivisibilities of labor and employment adjustment costs c) the issue of preferences, the non-separability of leisure and durable goods and d) the issue of serial correlation in the productivity growth. From this research two important properties emerge. First, the fact that there exist transitory dynamics as the economy adjusts consumption, investment and work effort in the process of moving towards a new steady state. In this period of adjustment the great ratios are expected to change temporarily. Second, there exists a common stochastic trend in consumption, investment and output due to the stochastic trend in productivity. These two issues can be examined in terms of cointegration tests between consumption, investment and output and in the case that there is empirical evidence that cointegration does exist, the short-run adjustment dynamics can be studied using vector error correction models (VECM). In other systems where $\mathbf{X}_t$ is augmented to include both the real variables, consumption, investment and output and nominal variables such as money balances, the

114

price level and the nominal interest rate, now $\mathbf{X_t} = [c_t, i_t, m_t - p_t, y_t, R_t]$ and if $m_t - p_t$, and R_t are I(1) then according to the theory I would expect to find three cointegrating vectors, the two great ratios: $\alpha = [1,0,0,-1,0]$, $\beta = [0,1,0,-1,0]$ and the money demand relation $\gamma = [0,0,1,-\gamma_4, \gamma_4]$. In this case $m_t - p_t$ represents the logarithm of real money balances and R_t is the nominal interest rate. According to the theory I expect $\gamma_4 = -1$ and γ_4 to be small and positive. These coefficients in the cointegrating vector for the money demand imply a one-to-one positive relation between real money balances and output and a small negative relation between real money balances and the nominal interest rate.

In this paper I will use the latest developments in the field of non-stationary variables and cointegration to test whether the data support the above cointegrating relations predicted by theory and if there is evidence for cointegration I will test whether the coefficients in the cointegrating relations are of the expected magnitude.

4.3 THE DATA AND TESTS FOR STOCHASTIC TRENDS

The data that are used in this paper are quarterly U.S. observations from 1960:1 to 1997:4. The variables are: real per capita personal consumption expenditures seasonally adjusted, c, real per capita private fixed investment seasonally adjusted, i, real per capita private GNP seasonally adjusted, y, defined as total GNP minus government expenditures. The real money balances variable is defined as per capita real money balances. The twelve different measures of money that are used in this paper are the Simple-Sum M1, M2, M3 and L denoted as S1 S2, S3 and SL respectively, the Divisia M1, M2, M3 and L denoted as D1 D2, D3 and DL and Currency Equivalence M1, M2, M3 and L measures denoted by C1, C2, C3, and CL. The interest rates that I use are 3-month treasury bill auction averages when a simple-sum or a currency-equivalence monetary aggregate is used. In the systems that involve the Divisia M1, Divisia M2, Divisia M3 and Divisia L monetary aggregates I use the more appropriate "user costs" of money, denoted by UC1, UC2, UC3, and UCL.

All variables are in logarithms with the exception of the nominal interest rates and the user costs of money. The real variables are produced using the GNP deflator as a price index.

4.3.1   Testing for Stochastic Trends in the Data

To test the cointegration properties of the data I need the variables to be non-stationary or I(1) in the Engle and Granger (1988) terminology. In Figure 4.1, I graph the logarithms of consumption, investment and output. Clearly all three variables show characteristic upward trends and cyclical effects. In Figures 4.2-4.5, I graph per capita real money balances from the narrowest definitions of the three monetary aggregates, Simple Sum, Divisia and Currency equivalence M1, to the broadest measures, L. Finally in Figure 4.6, I graph the great ratios c-y and i-y.

In order to test for cointegration we need consumption, investment, output, the twelve different measures of money and the interest rates and user costs to be non-stationary processes of the same order of integration. Also, according to the theory of balanced growth, we would expect that if consumption, investment and output have common stochastic trends, the great ratios must be stationary. Thus, evidence of non-stationarity of the great ratios is evidence against balanced growth theory.

For these reasons, it is important at this stage to examine the stationarity properties of the data and test for the presence of stochastic trends or unit roots. A stationary series has a constant mean and shocks to the series will not have permanent effects on the mean of the series. In this case the variable is mean reverting or stationary. Equivalently, a trend-stationary series follows a deterministic trend and any shocks to the variable will fade away and the variable will return to the original deterministic trend. In a series that has a stochastic trend or a unit root, a shock to the series at period t will have permanent effects. Such a series will have a non-stationary variance which will tend to infinity as $t \to \infty$.

In testing for stochastic trends (unit roots) in the log levels of the original data, I use two alternative testing procedures as an attempt to deal with the fact that some of the series may not be very informative about the existence or not of a unit root. In columns 2 and 3, of Table 4.1, I present the results of augmented Dickey-Fuller (ADF) tests[1] to the levels and first differences of the data respectively. In columns 4 and 5, I present the alternative non-parametric Phillips-Perron (PP) tests of Phillips and Perron (1988) for the existence of a unit root. The ADF tests are conducted using the following regression:

$$\Delta \log z_t = \alpha_0 + \alpha_1 t + \alpha_2 \log z_{t-1} + \sum_{i=1}^{m} \beta_i \Delta \log z_{t-i} + \varepsilon_t, \qquad (4.3.1)$$

where z_t is the series under consideration and m is selected large enough such that ε_t is white noise. The null hypothesis of a unit root is rejected if α_2 is negative and significantly different than zero. The critical values are not the usual t-statistics but are those given by Fuller (1976). The problem with this testing procedure is that the order of the autoregression is not known. One way to overcome this is to use some information criterion to select the best model. In this paper I use a lag order of m = 4 and the resulting Durbin-statistics show that any autocorrelation has been successfully removed. An alternative way to using the augmenting lags to correct for serial correlation is the Phillips-Peron testing procedure that uses non-parametric correction. The PP test involves estimating (4.3.1) with m = 0 and then the statistics are transformed to correct for serial

---

[1] See Dickey and Fuller (1981).

correlation in their asymptotic distribution. For the transformation formula see Phillips and Peron

(1988, Table 1, p. 308-9). The critical values for this test are the same as in the Dickey-Fuller tests.

The Newey and West (1987) method is used to estimate the error variance from the estimated

residuals as:

$$\frac{1}{N}\sum_{t=1}^{N}\varepsilon_t^2 + \frac{2}{N}\sum_{s=1}^{p}\omega(s,p)\sum_{t=s+1}^{N}\varepsilon_t\varepsilon_{t-s}, \qquad (4.3.2)$$

where p is the truncation lag parameter which is set in the estimation according to the Newey and

West suggested value, and $\omega(s,p) = \dfrac{1-s}{p+1}$.

According to the ADF tests, in panel A of Table 4.1, I find evidence that the three real

variables, the nominal interest rate, the user costs, S2, C1, C2, and C3 are all I(1), while the rest of

the monetary aggregates appear to be I(2). The consumption-output ratio and CL appear to be I(0)

or stationary. The PP tests, in panel B of Table 4.1, show that all variables are I(1) with the

exception of CL and the consumption-output great ratio which are I(0). Thus, in some cases the

data are not very informative about their stationarity properties and in column 6 of Table 4.1 I

report the decisions that are made regarding their order of integration. Whenever the ADF and the

PP tests produce conflicting results, I treat the respective variables as I(1) for the purposes of this

paper. Finally CL is found to be I(0) using both tests, so in the estimations where CL is included

the results must be interpreted with caution.

4.4 MAXIMUM LIKELIHOOD COINTEGRATION TESTS

In this section I will use the Johansen and Juselius (1992) maximum likelihood

cointegration tests to test for cointegration in three different systems. The first is the c, i, y system

where according to the theory I expect to find two cointegrating relations, namely the consumption-output and the investment-output great ratios. The second system that includes, m-p, y, and R, is estimated with each one of the twelve monetary aggregates. In this system I expect to identify one cointegrating vector that corresponds to the long-run money demand function. Finally in the third system I include all five variables, c, i, m-p, y and R expecting three common stochastic trends, the two great ratios and the money demand function.

4.4.1   The Econometric Framework

I follow Johansen and Juselius (1992) and for a system of p variables, I consider the following p-dimensional vector autoregressive model:

$$X_t = \sum_{i=1}^{k} \Pi_i X_{t-i} + \mu + \varepsilon_t \qquad (4.4.1)$$

where X_t is a vector of the variables that are included in the estimated system and ε_t is an independently and identically distributed p-dimensional vector of innovations with zero mean and covariance matrix Φ. If $\Pi = -(I - \Pi_1 - ... - \Pi_k)$ is the $p \times p$ total impact matrix I consider the hypothesis of the existence of a maximum of r<p cointegrating relations as

$$H_1(r) : \Pi = \alpha \beta' \qquad (4.4.2)$$

where α and β are $p \times r$ matrices of full rank. The β matrix is a matrix of cointegrating vectors such that $\beta' X_t$ is stationary even though X_t is itself non-stationary[2]. The α matrix is a matrix of error correction parameters.

The maximum likelihood estimation and the likelihood ratio test of this model has been investigated by Johansen (1988). According to Johansen and Juselius (1992) I transform equation (4.4.1) by subtracting X_{t-1} from both sides and collecting the terms on X_{t-1}. Then I add and subtract $(\Pi_1 - 1)X_{t-2}$ and repeat this procedure and collect terms to get:

$$\Delta X_t = \sum_{i=1}^{k-1} \Gamma_i \Delta X_{t-i} + \alpha \beta' X_{t-k} + \varepsilon_t \qquad (t = 1, \ldots, T) \qquad (4.4.3)$$

where

$$\Gamma_i = -(I - II_1 - \ldots - \Pi_i), \quad (i = 1, \ldots, k-1). \qquad (4.4.4)$$

In equation (4.4.3) the matrix Π is restricted as $\Pi = \alpha \beta'$ but the parameters vary independently. Thus, the parameters $\Gamma_1, \ldots, \Gamma_{k-1}$ can be eliminated by regressing ΔX_t and X_{t-k} on

---

[2] See Engle and Granger (1987).

lagged differences $\Delta X_{t-1},...,\Delta X_{t-k+1}$. These regressions produce the residuals R_{ot} and R_{kt} and residual product moment matrices

$$S_{ij} = T^{-1} \sum_{t=1}^{T} R_{it} R'_{jt} \quad (i,j = o,k).$$ \hfill (4.4.5)

The estimate of β is calculated[3] by solving the eigenvalue problem

$$\left| \lambda S_{kk} - S_{k0} S_{00}^{-1} S'_{k0} \right| = 0$$ \hfill (4.4.6)

for eigenvalues $\hat{\lambda}_1 > ... > \hat{\lambda}_p > 0$, eigenvectors $V = (\hat{v}_1,...,\hat{v}_p)$ normalized by $\hat{V}' S_{kk} \hat{V} = I$. The maximum likelihood estimators are given by

$$\hat{\beta} = (\hat{v}_1,...,\hat{v}_r), \qquad \hat{\alpha} = S_{0k} \hat{\beta} \qquad \text{and} \quad \hat{\Omega} = S_{\Omega\Omega} - \hat{\alpha}\hat{\alpha}'.$$ \hfill (4.4.7)

The maximized likelihood function is calculated from

_____

[3] See Johansen (1988).

121

$$L_{max}^{-2/T} = |\hat{\Omega}| = |S_{\Omega\Omega}| \prod_{i=1}^{r} (1 - \hat{\lambda}_i), \qquad (4.4.8)$$

and the likelihood ratio test of the hypothesis $H_1(r)$ is given by the trace test statistic or λ_{trace} :

$$-2\ln Q[H_1(r) \mid H_0] = -T \sum_{i=r+1}^{p} \ln(1 - \hat{\lambda}_i). \qquad (4.4.9)$$

An alternative test which is called the maximum eigenvalue test or λ_{max} is based on comparing $H_1(r-1)$ with $H_1(r)$:

$$-2\ln Q[H_1(r-) \mid H_1(r)] = -T\ln(1 - \hat{\lambda}_{r+1}). \qquad (4.4.10)$$

The critical values for these tests are given by Osterwald and Lenum (1990).

To select the appropriate lag order for each model in the corresponding VAR, I estimate VAR(k) models with k from 1 to 20 and select the order of the VAR that minimizes the Akaike Information Criterion (AIC). Using this criterion I select 3 lags for the c, i, y system, for the m-p, y, R system 6 lags are selected using the simple sum and currency equivalence monetary aggregates, while in using the Divisia aggregates I select a VAR(4) for Divisia M1 and a VAR(3) for the broader Divisia aggregates. The selection of the order of the VAR is important because the cointegration tests are quite sensitive to the order of the VARs.

4.4.2 Testing the c, i, y system

The first system that I am going to examine using the previously described Johansen methodology is the trivariate consumption, investment, and output system. I have already concluded in Section 4.3.1 that all three variables are non-stationary and I(1) so that we can use the cointegration analysis to test the theoretical proposition of balanced growth. According to the theory, the two great ratios, the consumption-output and investment-output ratios are expected to be stationary. Thus, if the theory is correct, I expect to find evidence of two cointegrating vectors. If the order of the variables in the system is $X_t = [c_t, i_t, y_t]$' then the two cointegrating vectors are expected to be: $\alpha = [1,0,-1]$ and $\beta = [0,1,-1]$ for the consumption and investment great ratios respectively, so that although the three variables are non-stationary there exists a linear combination of them that is stationary. The estimated λ_{max} and λ_{trace} test statistics and the corresponding null hypotheses that are calculated using an order 3 VAR are shown in Table 4.2. None of the two statistics is statistically significant at the 5% level. Thus, there is no evidence of any cointegrating relations in this system although the theory predicts two. Having in mind the unit root tests on the two great ratios, I was expecting to find one cointegrating relation. We have seen that the c-y variable that corresponds to the consumption-output great ratio was found to be stationary implying a long run relationship between the two I(1) variables. The trivariate cointegration test does not provide evidence for any cointegrating relations between the three variables.

4.4.3 The m-p, y, R System

The next system I am going to test is $X_t = [m - p, y, R]$. In this case I expect to find one cointegrating relationship according to theory, $[1, \beta_y, \beta_R]$, which corresponds to the long-run money demand function. If such a cointegrating vector exists I expect $\beta_y = -1$ and $\beta_R > 0$ and small.

This is because according to the theory output, y, must be positively related to the real money balances, m-p, and the relation must be one-to-one. Also, the interest rate elasticity, β_R, of real money balances must be negative and relatively small.

Here, for the real money balances variable, m-p, I use three different monetary aggregates: simple sum, Divisia, and currency equivalence. For all three aggregates I use four levels of aggregation, M1, M2, M3, and L, so that I test a total of 12 money measures. The variables are named such that S1 corresponds to the simple sum M1 measure, D1 refers to the Divisia M1 measure, C1 is the currency equivalence M1 and so on. For the nominal interest rate variable, R, in the case of the Divisia aggregates, I use the user cost of money which is a more appropriate measure of the opportunity cost of holding money for these aggregates. The results of the Johansen maximum likelihood cointegration tests are shown in Table 4.2. According to the λ_{max} and λ_{trace} statistics I find some evidence of cointegration at the 5% level, only when S1, S2, and D1 measures are used. In the other cases I accept the null hypothesis of no cointegration. Then, I impose some just-identifying restrictions for cointegration rank of r = 1 to identify the cointegrating vectors. In Table 4.3 I summarize the Johansen cointegration tests. The way these tests are constructed, a time trend is included in the cointegrating vectors. If the money demand function exists as predicted by the theory, there should be no trend in the cointegrating vectors. Thus, I test the null hypothesis that the time trend in each of the three cointegrating vectors is equal to zero, or that in the cointegrating vector [m-p,y,R,t], where t is the time trend, $\beta_4 = 0$. As we can see from Table 4.3, the null hypothesis that the time trend in the three cointegrating vectors is equal to zero, cannot be rejected at the 5% level. So, I impose next the over-identifying restriction that $\beta_4 = 0$ and the cointegrating vectors are identified as in Table 4.4. The coefficients of real money balances are normalized to 1. I observe that with the exception of the interest rate coefficient in the simple sum M2 cointegrating vector, all other coefficients have the correct signs. The coefficient on the interest rate or the user cost is positive and small as it is predicted by the theory, but the coefficients for the output elasticity of real money balances appear to be different than -1. Testing the overidentifying restriction that $\beta_2 = -1$, in column 5 of Table 4.3, I reject the null hypothesis for all three cointegrating vectors. Thus, I conclude that the coefficients on output are significantly greater than -1 so that the elasticity of real money balances to output is less than 1.

4.4.4   The c, i, m-p, y, R System

In this section I include all five variables in the same system so that now $X_t = [c, i, m\text{-}p, y, R]$. The cointegration tests are done using all twelve money measures. According to the theory I expect to find three cointegrating relations in this system, the two great ratios, and the money demand function. However, I have seen from the unit root tests that the investment-output great ratio, i-y, is nonstationary, so the one-to-one relation may not exist. Applying the Johansen methodology to test for cointegration in this system I get the results of Table 4.5. According to the λ_{max} and λ_{trace} test statistics, I cannot reject the null hypothesis of no cointegration or r = 0 for the cases of D2, D3, and C1. For all the other cases I find evidence of one cointegrating vector, with the exception of Divisia M1 where the λ_{max} test provides evidence of 3 cointegrating vectors, while the λ_{trace} test provides evidence for 2. According to Johansen (1991), this ambiguity is due to the low power in cases when the cointegration relation is quite close to the non-stationary boundary. However, since the λ_{trace} test takes into account all of the smallest eigenvalues it tends to have more power than the λ_{max} test. Thus, in the case of Divisia M1, I assume that there exist two cointegrating vectors. In column 3 of Table 4.6, I present the number of cointegrating vectors for each money measure. The next step is to identify the cointegrating vectors. Whenever r = 1 is selected, it is more likely that the one cointegrating vector is the long-run money demand function since from the trivariate c, i, y system I did not find any evidence of cointegration. Also, since we have seen that the c-y great ratio is stationary it is more likely that the consumption-output great ratio may have been picked up by the Johansen cointegration test. Thus, for the cases where $r = 1$, I test the overidentifying restrictions that $\beta_1 = \beta_2 = \beta_6 = 0$ and $\beta_2 = \beta_3 = \beta_5 = \beta_6 = 0$, that identify the long-run money demand function and the consumption-output great ratio respectively as the cointegrating vector. From Table 4.6, columns 4 and 5 we can see that I accept both hypotheses in the case of S1, but I reject them both for all the other money measures. The identified cointegrating vectors for S1 are shown in Table 4.7 in columns 2 and 3. Thus, although I find some evidence of one cointegrating vector in the S1 case, the tests cannot conclude whether that vector is one of the two cointegrating relations that I expect (consumption-output ratio or the money demand function), I fail to reject both null hypotheses.

The rejection of both cointegrating regressions for the other money measures means that the one cointegrating vector that the Johansen test detects is not the money demand or consumption great ratio that the theory predicts. For the case of Divisia M1, where we have two cointegrating vectors, I impose and test the overidentifying restriction that $\beta_2^1 = \beta_5^1 = \beta_6^1 = 0$ that identifies the consumption-output great ratio. This is distributed under the null as a χ^2 with 3 degrees of freedom. In column 6 of Table 4.6, we see that the null hypothesis cannot be rejected at the 5% level, and I find evidence that one cointegrating vector is the c-y ratio. In order to test jointly that the two identified cointegrating vectors are the c-y great ratio and the money demand function as predicted by the theory, I test the joint hypothesis that $\beta_2^1 = \beta_5^1 = \beta_6^1 = \beta_2^2 = \beta_6^2 = 0$. We can see in column 7 of Table 4.6 that the probability is 0.394 and I cannot reject the null hypothesis. The identified cointegrating vectors are shown in columns 4 and 5 of Table 4.7. The coefficient of y is expected to be equal to -1 in both cointegrating vectors. In the consumption-output cointegrating vector, in column 2 of Table 4.7, the coefficient of y is equal to -1.3860. The coefficient of y in the money demand cointegrating vector is equal to -0.4662. Although the coefficients are negative they do not seem to be jointly equal to -1 as I would expect in this system. The overidentifying restriction that the coefficients on income are both −1, or testing that $\beta_4^1 = \beta_4^2 = -1$, is strongly

rejected and the probability is 0.000. The coefficient of the user cost of money UC1, is positive and

small in size as expected, $\beta_5^2 = 0.0031$.

4.5 IMPULSE RESPONSES OF THE COINTEGRATING SYSTEMS

For the cases that I have found some evidence of cointegration will be interesting to see

how these cointegrating relations and the variables of the respective systems respond to various

shocks.

In the m-p, y, R system, I have identified the money demand function as a cointegrating

relation when I use simple sum M1, M2, and Divisia M1 as money measures. In Figures 4.7-4.9

we can see the persistence profile of system-wide shocks to the cointegrating vector for the S1, S2

and D1 cases respectively. We observe that a positive shock to the system is quite persistent on the

cointegrating vector and it is only absorbed after about 20 quarters for all three monetary

aggregates. In Figures 4.10-4.11 I present the impulse response of the cointegrating vectors to

shocks to specific variables of the system. In Figure 4.10, I shock real per capita output and in

panels A, B and C we can see the impulse responses for the case of S1, S2, and D1 respectively.

For S1 in panel A, the positive shock produces a positive response to the cointegrating relation for

the first 6 quarters and then it becomes negative. The effect of the shock when I use S2 and D1 is

quite different since the shock produces a negative response of the cointegrating vector for the first

quarters before it is absorbed. When the equation that is shocked is that of the real money balances

we see that this shock is absorbed in about 25 quarters for all three money measures but the shock

has a negative short-term effect to the cointegrating vector when D1 is used.

In the five variable system, the only case where I both found cointegrating relations and I was able to identify the expected by the theory cointegrating vectors, was when Divisia M1 was used as the monetary aggregate. In Figure 4.12 we see that a positive system-wide shock produces a positive shock to both identified cointegrating vectors. The biggest part of the shock is absorbed in the first 12 quarters but then the speed of adjustment to the respective long-run relations is very slow.

In Figure 4.13 I present the impulse response of the two cointegrating relations to a shock in the real per capita output. The consumption-output great ratio is below its long-run equilibrium for a period of about 10 quarters and then it slowly adjusts. The money demand relation does not show such a big impact but it oscillates around the long-run equilibrium, while both relations show long persistence. In Figures 4.14 and 4.15 we see that shocks to the real Divisia M1 money balances and the user cost of money affect the money demand cointegrating relation more that the consumption-output great ratio and both cointegrating vectors tend, although slowly, to return to their long-run equilibria.

Finally, it is interesting to see what are the effects of different shocks to the system's variables. In Figures 4.16 and 4.17 I present the impulse responses of those variables to one standard deviation shocks to real per capita output and real money balances. The output shock produces a positive response to all the other variables at the impact period but this positive effect dies out and becomes permanently negative after about 8 periods, with the exception of money balances that seems to be negative from the beginning. In the case of an one standard deviation shock to the money demand equation, we can see in Figure 4.17 that investment and output respond positively in the first 10 quarters, then the effect becomes negative for about 8 quarters but they return to the positive territory and stay there permanently. The impulse response of consumption to the one standard deviation shock to the real money balances is positive for all periods.

The impulse responses in Figures 4.16 and 4.17, are consistent with what I expected from economic theory and econometrics of non-stationary variables. We see that for both the real per capita output and the real balances shock, the most volatile variable of the system is investment. Also, consumption appears to be at least volatile variable which is consistent with the permanent income hypothesis. Individuals spread the effects of the shocks over many periods decreasing the volatility of per capita real consumption.

Finally, from Figures 4.7-4.17, we see that, in general, although slowly, the cointegrating relations tend to revert to their long run equilibria, while the specific variables seem to be permanently affected by shocks to the system. This of course is expected, as in section 4.3.1 I have concluded that the variables are I(1) or non-stationary. The important property of integrated variables is that a shock will permanently affect their levels - they do not revert to a constant mean or a deterministic trend.

4.6 CONCLUSIONS

According to the balanced growth theory, as we have seen, the great ratios are expected to be stationary. In this paper, using a simple real business cycle model of the general class proposed by Kydland and Prescott (1982) and where total factor productivity evolves according to a random walk with drift process, I tested the stationarity of the great ratios. Evidence against the stationarity of the great ratios is evidence against the balanced growth theory. The necessary but not sufficient condition for a number of series to be cointegrated is that all the series in question are integrated of the same order of integration. Applying the Dickey-Fuller (1981) and Phillips-Perron (1988) tests for unit roots I concluded that all series have a unit root or they are I(1) according to the Engle and Granger (1988) terminology with the exception of CL, the currency equivalence L money measure, and c-y, the consumption-output great ratio which were found to be stationary or I(0).

In Section 4.4.2, I use the real variable system [c, i, y] and apply the Johansen and Juselius (1992) maximum likelihood cointegration testing procedure. Although, the theory predicts two cointegrating vectors, I do not find evidence for any such vectors, not even the c-y great ratio that was found to be stationary as we have seen before.

In Section 4.4.3, where I use the system [m-p, y, R], I expected to find one cointegrating vector, the money demand function. There is evidence of one cointegrating relationship only when S1, S2 and D1 are used as monetary aggregates. The coefficients of the interest rates on the identified cointegrated vectors are as expected small and positive with the exception of S2 where it is negative. The coefficients on output are all negative as money demand theory suggests but the elasticity of real money balances with respect to output is significantly greater than −1.

In the system where I include all five variables [c, i, m-p, y, R], in Section 4.4.4, the theory predicts three cointegrated vectors, the two great ratios and the money demand function. The ML cointegration tests show no cointegrated vectors when D2, D3, and C1 are used as monetary aggregates, two when D1 is used and one with all other measures. In the case of D1, the joint hypothesis that the two cointegrating vectors are the money demand function and the consumption-output great ratio cannot be rejected and when these two vectors are identified, the coefficient of the user cost of money is small and positive as predicted, the coefficients of output have the correct sign but are different than −1.

Thus, the cointegrating vectors that I both identified and they are consistent with the theory are the money demand function in the [m-p, y, R] system when M1, M2 and D1 is used, and in the [c, i, m-p, y, R] system, the consumption-output great ratio and the money demand function when D1 is used. The impulse responses of those cointegrating vectors to system wide shocks and to shocks to specific variables of interest in general are consistent with the theory. The cointegrating vectors show long persistence but they return to their long-run equilibria. The specific series are permanently affected by the shock as it is expected for non-stationary variables.

Summarizing, the only cases where I find evidence of cointegrating vectors that are predicted by the theory is when simple sum M1, simple sum M2 or Divisia M1 monetary aggregates are used. Thus, the theory is not supported at all by these data when broader measures of money are used, and there is some evidence that the theory is correct when the narrowest of the money measures are used. The results appear not to be sensitive to the different monetary aggregates as in simple sum, Divisia or currency equivalent, but to how broad the specific money measure is.

TABLE 4.1

Variable	A. Augmented Dickey-Fuller			B. Phillips-Peron Test		Decision
	Level	1st Diff.		Level	1st Diff.	
			Real Variables			
c	-3,14	-4,84		-2,11	-10,56	I(1)
i	-2,82	-4,93		-1,99	-6,91	I(1)
y	-4,16	-5,51		-2,90	-8,94	I(1)
			Monetary Aggregates			
S1	-2,18	-2,88		-1,55	-5,18	I(1)
S2	-2,46	-3,53		-1,79	-5,50	I(1)
S3	-2,27	-2,96		-1,44	-4,29	I(1)
SL	-2,65	-2,84		-1,34	-4,05	I(1)
D1	-2,23	-2,98		-1,54	-5,18	I(1)
D2	-2,49	-3,30		-1,86	-4,68	I(1)
D3	-2,62	-3,16		-1,93	-4,21	I(1)
DL	-3,13	-3,33		-2,08	-4,11	I(1)
C1	-1,83	-4,27		-1,55	-9,12	I(1)
C2	-3,34	-5,94		-3,36	-11,45	I(1)
C3	-3,35	-6,00		-3,36	-10,99	I(1)
CL	-3,56	-5,94		-3,50	-10,89	I(0)
			Interest Rate and User Costs			
R	-2,23	-4,00		-2,11	-9,98	I(1)
UC1	-1,56	-5,03		-1,72	-12,13	I(1)
UC2	-2,23	-5,57		-2,25	-11,85	I(1)
UC3	-2,27	-5,82		-2,27	-11,62	I(1)
UCL	-2,27	-5,92		-2,28	-11,62	I(1)
			Great Ratios			
c-y	-4,23	-		-3,50	-	I(0)
i-y	-2,01	-4,58		-1,48	-10,71	I(1)

The 95% critical value for the tests is -3.44

TABLE 4.2

JOHANSEN ML COINTEGRATION TESTS

Null Hypothesis	λ_{max}	λ_{trace}	Null Hypothesis	λ_{max}	λ_{trace}
	System c, i, y			System SL, y, R	
r = 0	24,0968	31,1647	r = 0	19,3580	39,9943
r <= 1	5,1422	7,0679	r <= 1	15,1258	20,6363
r <= 2	1,9257	1,9257	r <= 2	5,5105	5,5105
	System s1, y, R			System D1, y, UC1	
r = 0	22,8295	42.9696*	r = 0	25,1522	51.4949*
r <= 1	14,2367	20,1400	r <= 1	20.6393*	26.3427*
r <= 2	5,9034	5,9034	r <= 2	5,7034	5,7034
	System S2, y, R			System D2, y, UC2	
r = 0	25,2199	44.1327*	r = 0	20,6617	37,2747
r <= 1	13,9636	18,9128	r <= 1	8,6274	16,6131
r <= 2	4,9492	4,9492	r <= 2	7,9857	7,9857
	System S3, y, R			System D3, y, UC3	
r = 0	17,9820	36,9006	r = 0	22,3035	38,1343
r <= 1	14,7247	18,9186	r <= 1	9,4971	15,8308
r <= 2	4,1939	4,1939	r <= 2	6,3337	6,3337

* Statistically significant at the 5% level.

TABLE 4.2 (CONTINUED)

Null Hypothesis	λ_{max}	λ_{trace}	Null Hypothesis	λ_{trace}
	System DL, y, UCL			
$= 0$	24,8582	39,7429	$r = 0$	35,9516
≤ 1	9,2373	14,8848	$r \leq 1$	19,0849
≤ 2	5,6475	5,6475	$r \leq 2$	6,8046
	System C1, y, R			
$= 0$	19,8895	37,1179	$r = 0$	35,8469
≤ 1	13,2308	17,2284	$r \leq 1$	18,7241
≤ 2	3,9976	3,9976	$r \leq 2$	6,4875
	System C2, y, R			
$= 0$	16,3343	34,9992		
≤ 1	11,6640	18,6650		
≤ 2	7,0010	7,0010		

Statistically significant at the 5% level.

TABLE 4.3

MULTIVARIATE HYPOTHESIS TESTING

System	VAR order	Coint. Vectors	H_0: Trend = 0 (Prob.)
c, i, y	3	0	-

Système m-p, y,
R

Monetary Aggregate	VAR order	Coint. Vectors	H_0: Trend = 0 (Prob.)	H_0: $\beta_y = -1$ (Prob.)
S1	6	1	0,460	0,000
S2	6	1	0,172	0,000
S3	6	0	-	-
SL	6	0	-	-
D1	4	2	0,080	0,000
D2	3	0	-	-
D3	3	0	-	-
DL	3	0	-	-
C1	6	0	-	-
C2	6	0	-	-
C3	6	0	-	-
CL	6	0	-	-

TABLE 4.4

ESTIMATES OF COINTEGRATED VECTORS

Variable	Monetary Aggregate		
	Sum M1	Sum M2	Divisia M1
m-p	1,0000 (normalized)	1,0000 (normalized)	1,0000 (normalized)
Y	-0,3118 (0.0540)	-0,5938 (0.1381)	-0,4513 (0.0766)
R	0,0387 (0.0044)	-0,0224 (0.0079)	0,0032 (0.00001)

Note: the numbers in parentheses are standard errors.

TABLE 4.5

JOHANSEN ML COINTEGRATION TESTS

Null Hypothesis	λ_{max}	λ_{trace}	Null Hypothesis	λ_{max}	λ_{trace}
	System c, i, S1, y, R			System c, i, SL, y, R	
r = 0	31,5090	92.4096*	r = 0	39.5728*	93.3766*
r <= 1	28,2196	60,9006	r <= 1	21,9276	53,8038
r <= 2	19,6582	32,6811	r <= 2	16,8483	31,8762
r <= 3	10,3509	13,0229	r <= 3	8,7745	15,0279
r <= 4	2,6720	2,6720	r <= 4	6,2534	6,2534
	System c, i, S2, y, R			System c, i, D1, y, UC1	
r = 0	33,8207	90.6507*	r = 0	33,3307	101.6186*
r <= 1	23,8877	56,8300	r <= 1	31,4833	68.2879*
r <= 2	19,4602	32,9423	r <= 2	25.9482*	36,8046
r <= 3	9,8658	13,4821	r <= 3	8,0636	10,8563
r <= 4	3,6163	3,6163	r <= 4	2,7928	2,7928
	System c, i, S3, y, R			System c, i, D2, y, UC2	
r = 0	33,0894	88.8732*	r = 0	36,2285	83,1006
r <= 1	22,1154	55,7838	r <= 1	22,3939	46,8721
r <= 2	20,1947	33,6684	r <= 2	12,0365	24,4782
r <= 3	9,5318	13,4738	r <= 3	7,2629	12,4417
r <= 4	3,9419	3,9419	r <= 4	5,1788	5,1788

* Statistically significant at the 5% level.

TABLE 4.5 (CONTINUED)

JOHANSEN ML COINTEGRATION TESTS

Null Hypothesis	λ_{max}	λ_{trace}	Null Hypothesis	λ_{max}	λ_{trace}
	System c, i, D3, y, UC3			System c, i, C2, y, R	
r = 0	37,3855	84,0647	r = 0	43.6680*	101.9456*
r <= 1	23,3814	46,6791	r <= 1	24,5939	58,2776
r <= 2	11,8005	23,2977	r <= 2	19,0078	33,6838
r <= 3	7,4843	11,4972	r <= 3	11,3930	14,6760
r <= 4	4,0129	4,0129	r <= 4	3,2830	3,2830
	System c, i, DL, y, UCL			System c, i, C3, y, UC1	
r = 0	42.4736*	88.9939*	r = 0	45.0046*	103.3418*
r <= 1	22,7414	46,5203	r <= 1	23,8950	58,3372
r <= 2	12,1491	23,7788	r <= 2	19,1063	34,4421
r <= 3	7,9328	11,6297	r <= 3	12,2848	15,3358
r <= 4	3,6969	3,6969	r <= 4	3,0510	3,0510
	System c, i, C1, y, R			System c, i, CL, y, UC2	
r = 0	37,0042	82,4623	r = 0	44.0516*	101.3749*
r <= 1	20,1174	45,4581	r <= 1	23,3970	57,3234
r <= 2	15,3289	25,3407	r <= 2	18,9397	33,9264
r <= 3	7,8310	10,0118	r <= 3	12,0846	14,9867
r <= 4	2,1808	2,1808	r <= 4	2,9022	2,9022

* Statistically significant at the 5% level.

TABLE 4.6

MULTIVARIATE HYPOTHESIS TESTING IN THE c, i, m-p, y, R SYSTEM

Monetary Aggregate	VAR order	r	$\beta_1 = \beta_2 = \beta_6 = 0$	$\beta_2 = \beta_3 = \beta_5 = \beta_6 = 0$	$\beta_2^1 = \beta_5^1 = \beta_6^1 = 0$	$\beta_2^2 = \beta_3^2 = \beta_5^2 = \beta_2^2 = \beta_6^2 = 0$
				Hypotheses Testing		
S1	6	1	0,088	0,596		
S2	6	1	0,045	0,017		
S3	6	1	0,009	0,021		
SL	6	1	0,002	0,001		
D1	6	2	.	.	0,618	0,394
D2	6	0	.	.		
D3	6	0	.	.		
DL	6	1	0,000	0,001		
C1	6	0	.	.		
C2	6	1	0,000	0,002		
C3	6	1	0,000	0,001		
CL	6	1	0,000	0,001		

Note: r is the number of cointegrating vectors. The numbers in hypothesis testing are probabilities.For the Divisia monetary aggregates R refers to the corresponding user costs.

TABLE 4.7

ESTIMATES OF COINTEGRATED VECTORS

ble	Monetary Aggregate is S1		Monetary Aggregate is D1	
	Consumption-Output	Money Demand	Consumption-Output	Money Demand
	1,0000 (normalized)	0,0000 (restricted)	1,0000 (normalized)	0,0000 (restricted)
	0,0000 (restricted)	0,0000 (restricted)	0,0000 (restricted)	0,0000 (restricted)
	0,0000 (restricted)	1,0000 (normalized)	0,0000 (restricted)	1,0000 (normalized)
	-1,3874 (0.0266)	-0,3753 (0.0594)	-1,3860 (0.0274)	-0,4662 (0.0624)
	0,0000 (restricted)	0,0406 (0.0041)	0,0000 (restricted)	0,0031 (0.000003)
	0,0000 (restricted)	0,0000 (restricted)	0,0000 (restricted)	0,0000 (restricted)

the numbers in parentheses are standard errors.

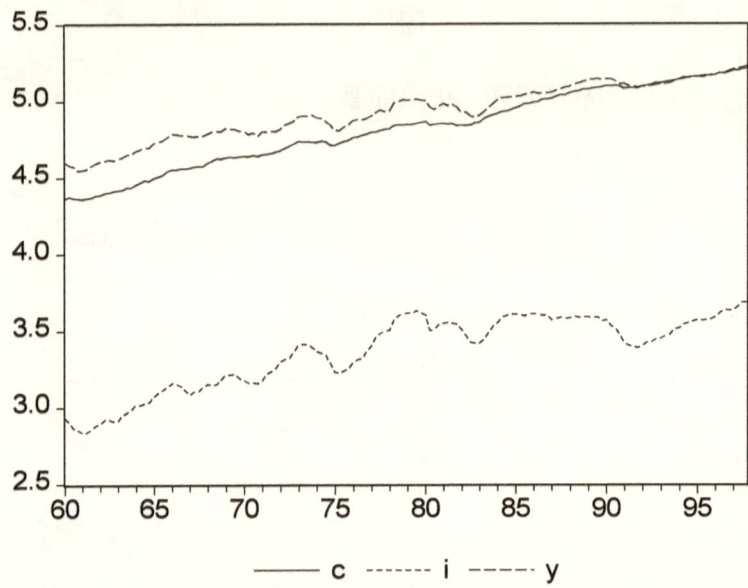

Figure 4.1. The Logarithms of Consumption Investment and Output

—— c ------ i ----- y

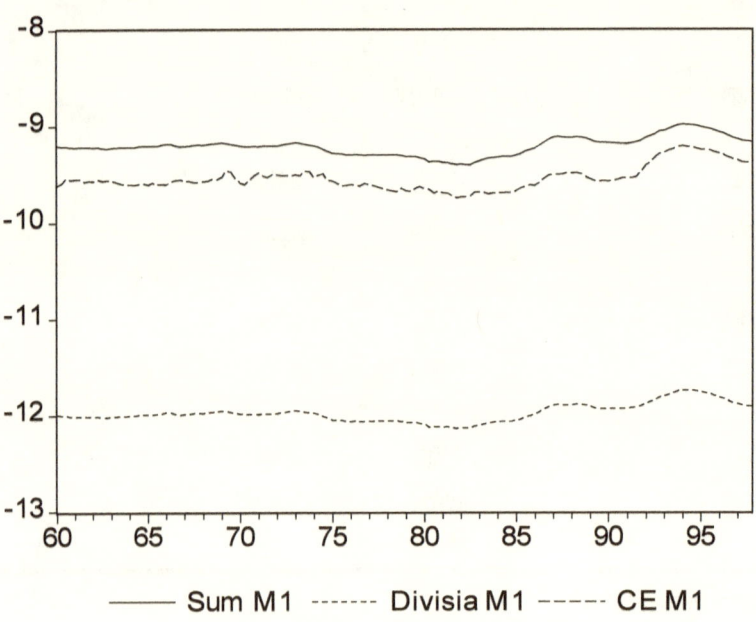

Figure 4.2. Simple-Sum M1, Divisia M1 and Currency Equivalence M1

—— Sum M1 ------ Divisia M1 ----- CE M1

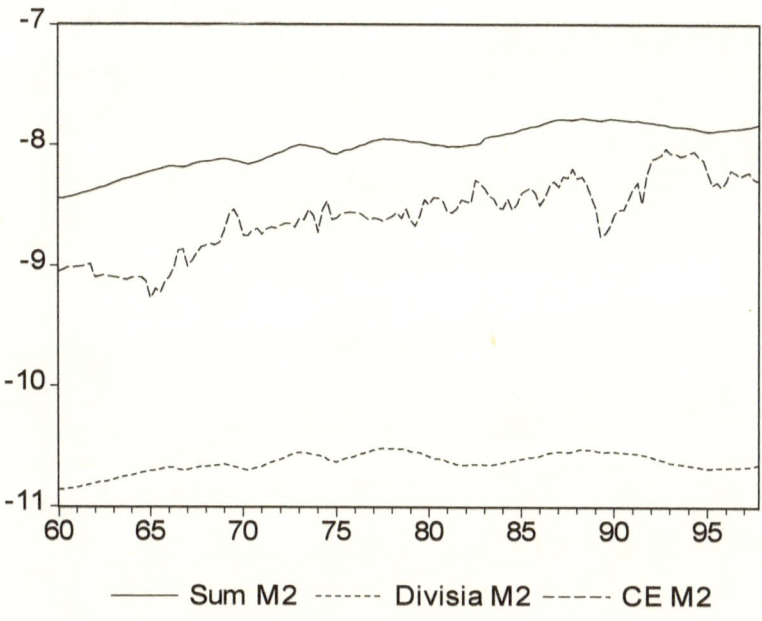

Figure 4.3. Simple-Sum M2, Divisia M2 and Currency Equivalence M2

—— Sum M2   ------ Divisia M2   ----- CE M2

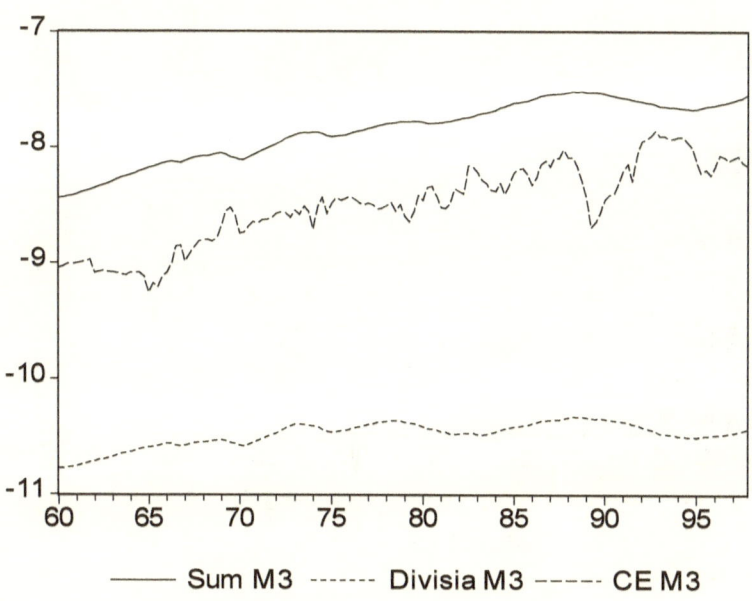

Figure 4.4. Simple-Sum M3, Divisia M3 and Currency Equivalence M3

—— Sum M3   ------ Divisia M3   ----- CE M3

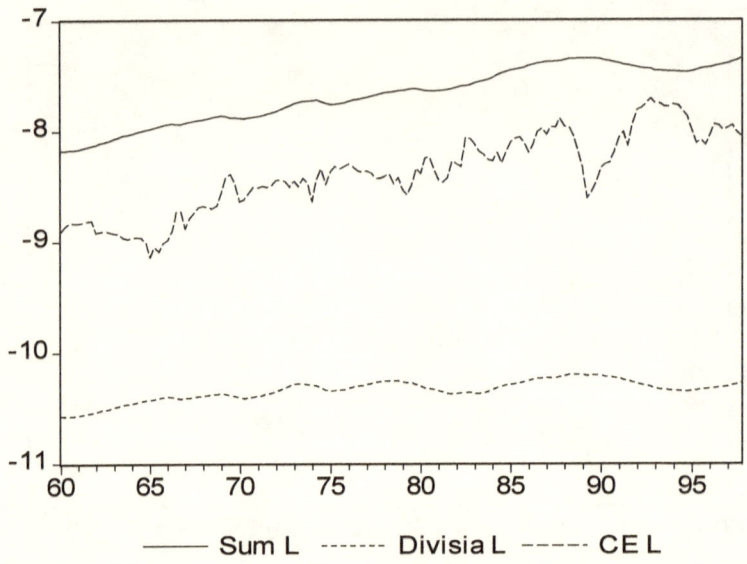

Figure 4.5. Simple-Sum L, Divisia L and Currency Equivalence L

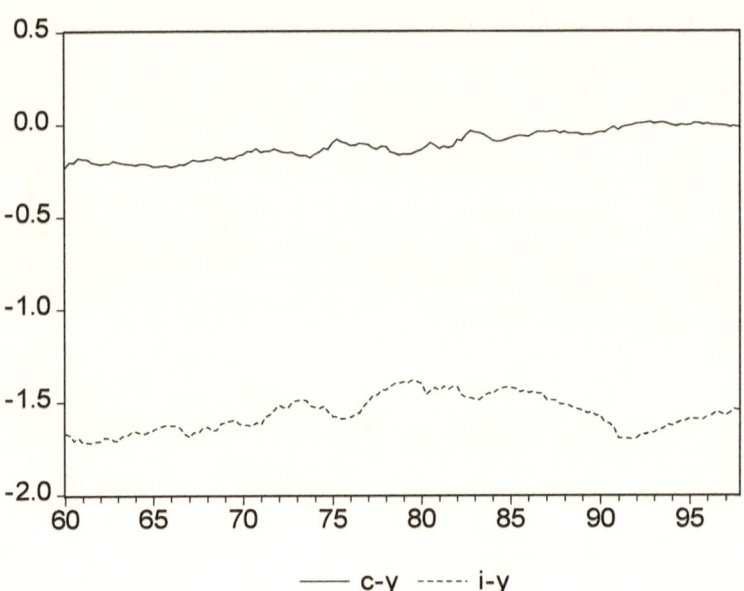

Figure 4.6. The y-c and i-c great ratios

Figure 4.7. Cointegrating Vector with Sum M1

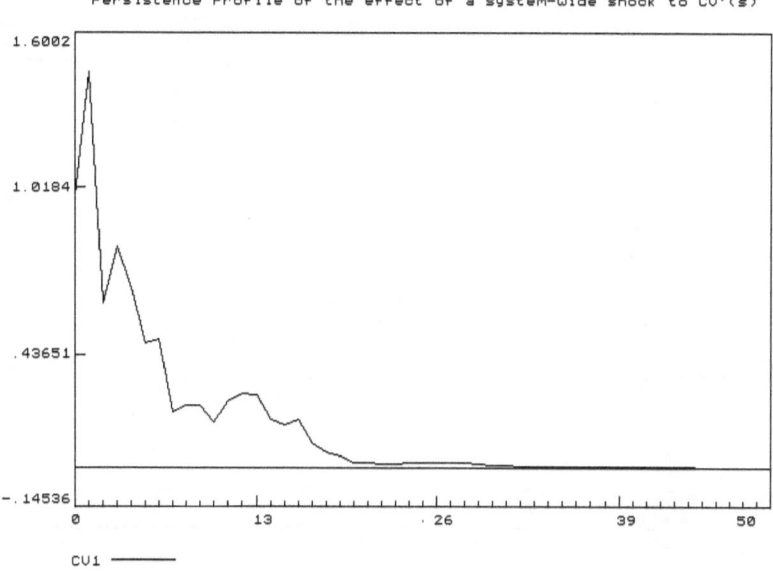

Figure 4.8. Cointegrating Vector with Sum M2

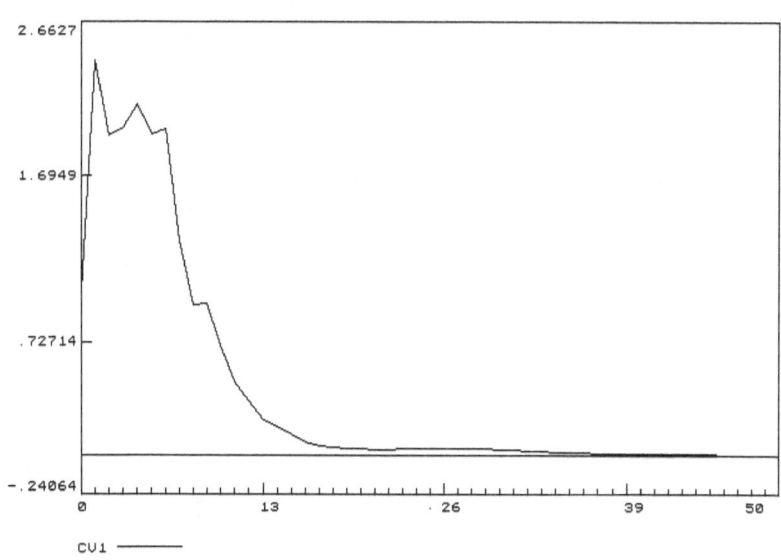

Figure 4.9. Cointegrating Vector with Divisia M1

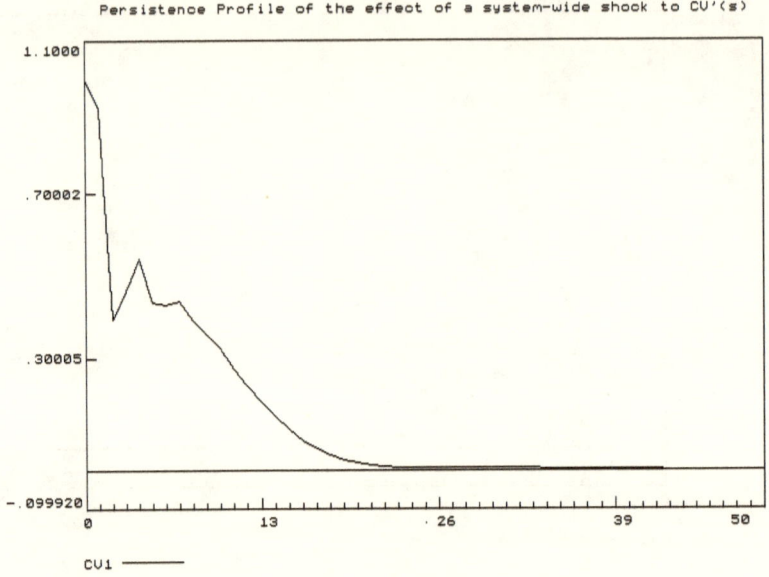

Persistence Profile of the effect of a system-wide shock to CV'(s)

CV1 ————

145

Figure 4.10. Cointegrating Vector IR to y
A. m-p = Sum M1

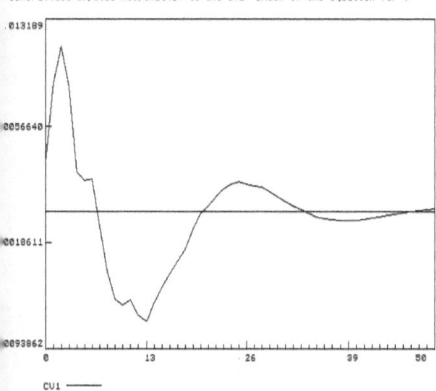

Figure 4.11. Cointegrating Vector IR to m-p
A. m-p = Sum M1

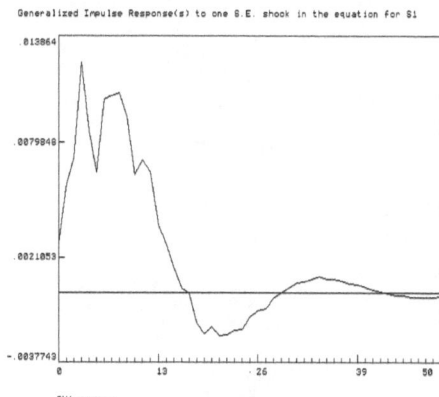

B. m-p = Sum M2

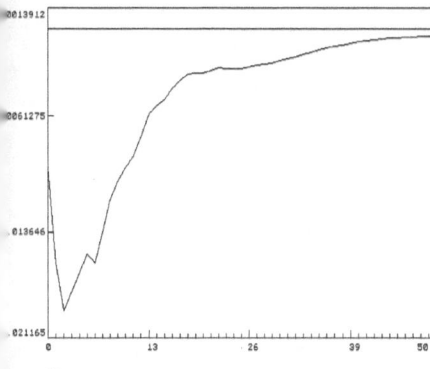

B. m-p = Sum M2

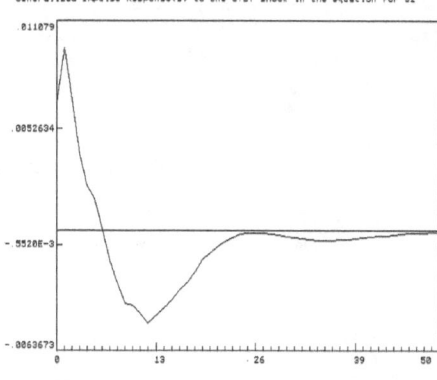

C. m-p = Divisia M1

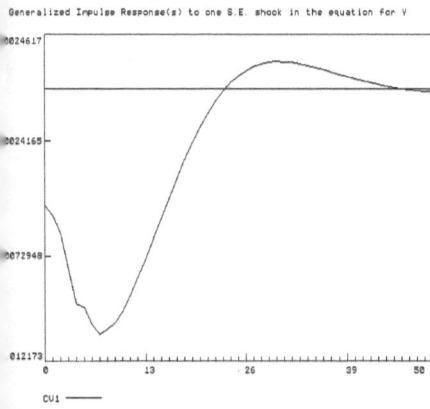

C. m-p = Divisia M1

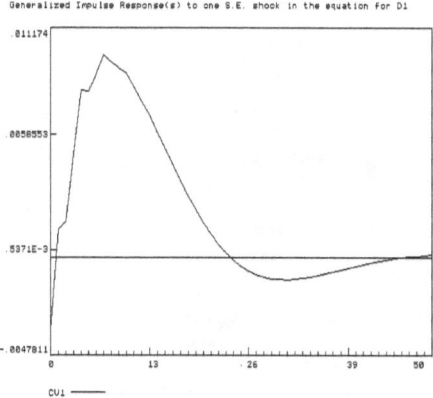

146

Figure 4.12. Persistence of C.V.'s to System-Wide Shocks

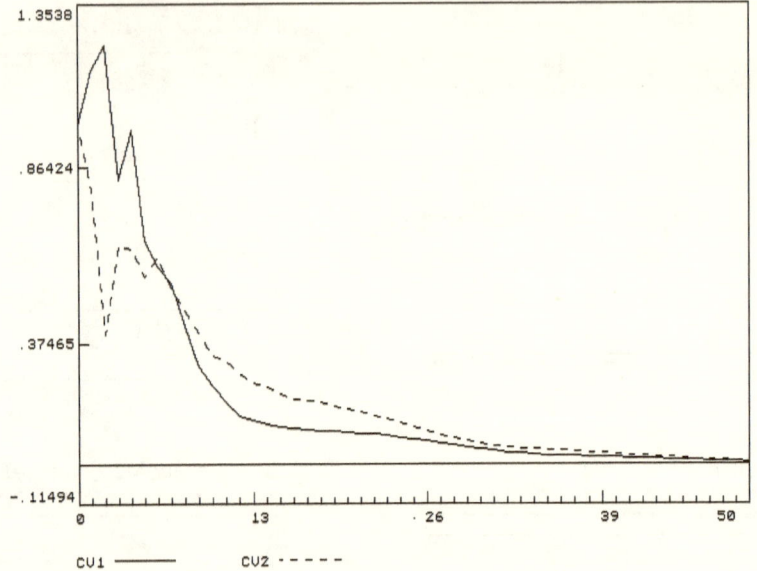

Persistence Profile of the effect of a system-wide shock to CV'(s)

Figure 4.13. Impulse Response of C.V.'s to Output Shocks

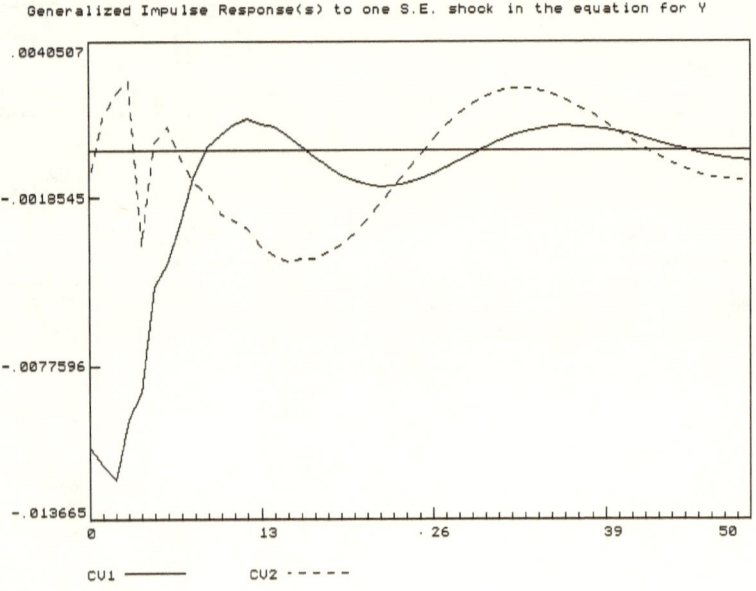

Generalized Impulse Response(s) to one S.E. shock in the equation for Y

Figure 4.14. Impulse Response of C.V.'s to Real Money Balances Shocks

Generalized Impulse Response(s) to one S.E. shock in the equation for D1

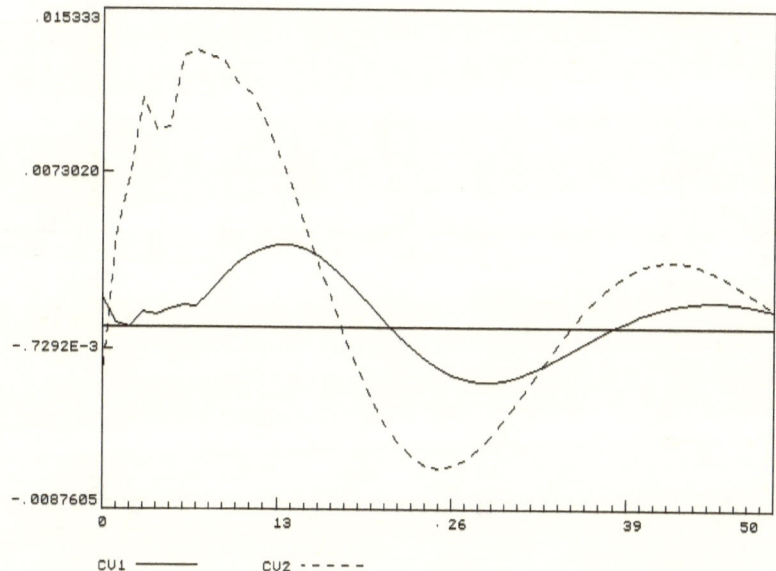

Figure 4.15. Impulse Response of C.V.'s to User Cost of Money Shocks

Generalized Impulse Response(s) to one S.E. shock in the equation for UC1

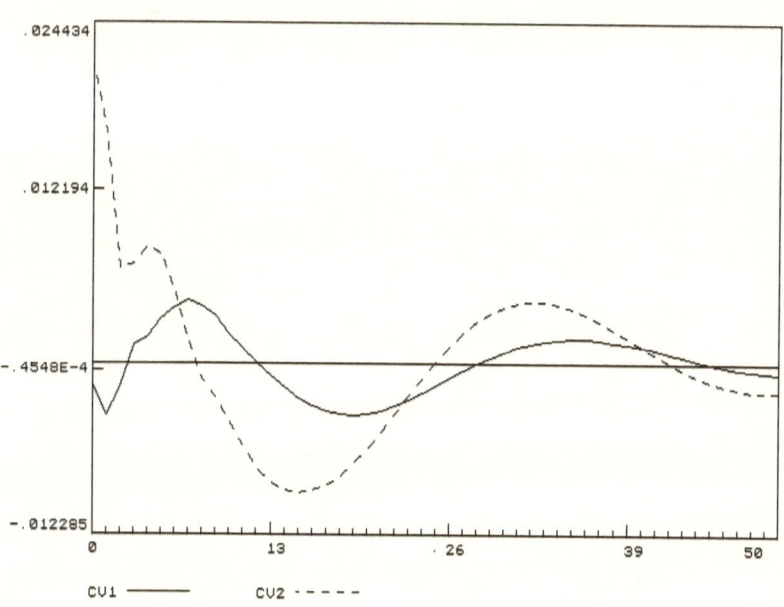

148

Figure 4.16. Impulse Responses to Output Shocks

Generalized Impulse Response(s) to one S.E. shock in the equation for Y

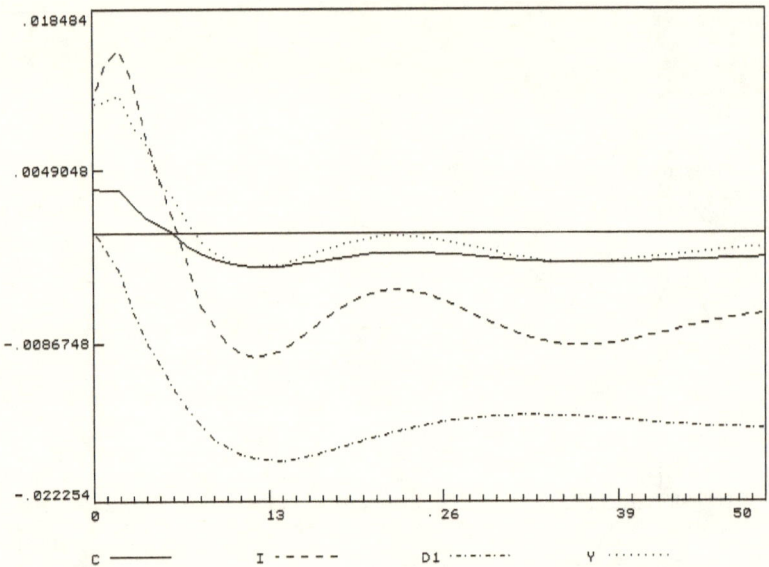

Figure 4.17. Impulse Responses to Real Money Balances Shocks

Generalized Impulse Response(s) to one S.E. shock in the equation for D1

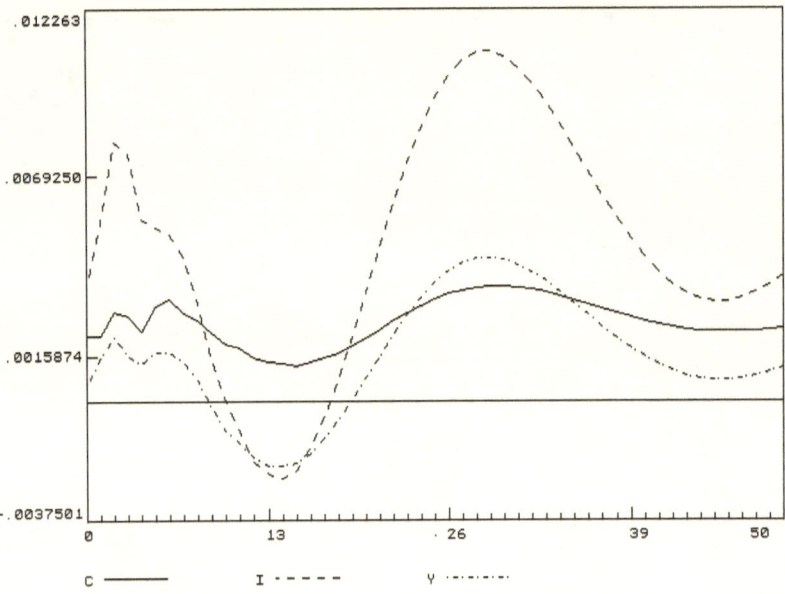

CHAPTER 5

CONCLUSION

In chapter 2 of this thesis, I have tested the absolute purchasing power parity theory in 17 countries using the Fisher and Seater (1993) and King and Watson (1997) testing methodologies. Although, in the literature, little evidence is found in support of PPP, the results using the long-run derivative and the long-run multiplier in Chapter 2 of this thesis, provide strong evidence that PPP holds in the long run. Most of the researchers that deal with the theory of PPP, perceive the lack of cointegration between the relative price ratio and the exchange rate as a point where testing has to stop, since this is treated as evidence that PPP does not hold and the testing stops at that point. In this thesis, after testing for the time series properties of the series, I tested for cointegration. In the case where the series would have been found to have a common stochastic trend, PPP testing would have taken a different direction. I would examine whether the coefficients of the cointegrating vector satisfy the requirements for PPP to hold, that is, the coefficient on the relative price ratio should be equal to 1, and also test causality, such that innovations in the relative price, cause the innovations in the exchange rate, if PPP holds. Rejecting cointegration, I was able to use the Fisher and Seater (1993) and King and Watson (1997) tests. Cointegration is not a necessary nor a sufficient condition for PPP to hold.

In Chapter 3, I model the historical evolution of six energy future prices, in an effort to produce in sample forecasts of the mean and volatility of these series. Visual inspection of the series and formal testing, made evident the presence of volatility clustering and a time-varying heteroscedasticity. The selection of the optimum lag structure in the autoregressive representation of the series, ensured that no linear dependencies were present in the error term. The best fitted model for the conditional variance was then selected to account for nonlinear processes in the disturbance terms. The actual values of the series were lying within the 95% confidence band constructed with the conditional variance. I also showed that the forecast errors and the forecast variance are smaller using the conditional variance in short-term forecasts, than using the unconditional one. This of course happens because the unconditional variance is characterized by

151

long memory relative to the conditional one. The unconditional variance puts the same weight to shocks that happened many periods in the past, while conditional variance weights more heavily recent realizations of the variable in question.

In Chapter 4, I test the balanced growth theory and the existence of a stable money demand function. This is done using three different monetary aggregation procedures, the simple sum, Divisia, and currency equivalent. It is interesting to see if the results of these tests are sensitive to the monetary aggregate that is used. Most of the variables of the system are found to be nonstationary, and thus, the Johansen and Juselius (1992) maximum likelihood cointegration test is used to identify in the system the cointegrating vectors that are predicted by the balanced growth and monetary theory. Cointegrating vectors that are predicted by the theory are only identified when the simple sum M1, simple sum M2, and Divisia M1 monetary aggregates where used. According to these findings, the results appear not to be sensitive to the monetary aggregate that is used but to the level of aggregation. The narrowest money specifications seem to better support the theory.

REFERENCES

Adler, Michael and Lehman, Bruce. "Deviations from Purchasing Power Parity in the Long Run." *Journal of Finance* 38 (1983), 1471-1487.

Akaike, H. (1974), "A New Look at the Statistical Model Identification", IEEE Transactions on Automatic Control, 19, p. 716-723.

Baillie, R.T., and Bollerslev, T. (1989), "The Message in Daily Exchange Rates: A Conditional-Variance Tale", *Journal of Business and Economic Statistics*, 7, p. 297-305.

Black, F. (1976), "Studies of Stock Price Volatility Changes", *Proceedings of the 1976 Meeting of Business and Economic Statistics Section*, American Statistical Association, p. 177-181.

Bollerslev, T. (1986), "Generalized Autoregressive Conditional Heteroscedasticity", *Journal of Econometrics*, 31, p. 307-327.

Chrystal, Alec K. and MacDonald Ronald. "Empirical Evidence on the Recent Behavior and Usefulness of Simple Sum and Weighted Measures of the Money Stock". The Federal Reserve Bank of St.Louis Review 76, no. 2 (1994), 73-109.

Coe, Patrick and Serletis, Apostolos. "Bounds Tests of the Theory of Purchasing Power Parity." University of Calgary, Mimeo (2000).

Dickey, David A. and Fuller, Wayne A. "Likelihood Ratio Statistics for Autoregressive Time Series With a Unit Root." *Econometrica* 49 (1981), 1057-1072.

Diebold, Francis.X. (1998), *Elements of Forecasting*, South-Western College Publishing.

Diebold, Francis X., Husted, Stephen and Rush, Mark. "Real Exchange Rates Under the Gold Standard." *Journal of Political Economy* 99 (1991), 1252-1271.

Dueker, Michael and Serletis, Apostolos. "Do Real Exchange Rates Have Autoregressive Unit Roots? A Test Under the Alternative of Long Memory and Breaks." The University of Calgary, mimeo (1997).

Enders, Walter. (1995), *Applied Econometric Time Series*, John Wiley.

Engle, Robert.F. (1982), "Autoregressive Conditional Heteroscedasticity with Estimates of the Variance of U.K. Inflation", *Econometrica*, 50, p. 987-1008.

Engle, Robert.F., Lilien, David, and Robins, Russel. (1987), "Estimating Time Varying Risk Premia in the Term Structure: The ARCH-M Model", *Econometrica*, 55, p. 391-407.

Engle, Robert F. and Granger, Clive W. "Cointegration and Error Correction: Representation, Estimation and Testing." *Econometrica* 55 (1987), 251-276.

Fisher, Mark E. and Seater, John J. "Long-Run Neutrality and Superneutrality in an ARIMA Framework." *American Economic Review* 83 (1993), 402-415.

Flynn, Alston N., and Boucer, Janice L. " Tests of Long-Run Purchasing Power Parity Using Alternative Methodologies." *Journal of Macroeconomics* 15 (1993), 109-122.

Frenkel, Jacob. "Purchasing Power Parity: Doctrinal Perspective and Evidence from the 1920s." *Journal of International Economics* 8 (1980), 169-191.

Fuller, W.A. (1976), *Introduction to Statistical Time Series*, New York: John Wiley & Sons.

Geweke, J., and Meese, R. (1981), "Estimating Regression Models of Finite but Unknown Order", *International Economic Review*, 22, p. 55-60.

Glen, Jack D. "Real Exchange Rates in the Short, Medium, and Long Run." *Journal of International Economics* 33 (1992), 147-166.

Grilli, Vittorio and Kaminsky, Graciela. "Nominal Exchange Rate Regimes and the Real Exchange Rate: Evidence from the United States and Great Britain, 1885-1986." *Journal of Monetary Economics* 27 (1991), 191-212.

Higgins, Matthew L., and Bera, Anil K. (1992), "A Class of Nonlinear ARCH Models", *International Economic Review*, 33, p. 137-158.

Hsieh, David A. (1989), "Modeling Heteroscedasticity in Daily Foreign-Exchange Rates", *Journal of Business and Economic Statistics*, 7, p. 307-317.

IMF, International Fianancial Statistics.

Johansen, Soren. "Statistical Analysis of Cointegration Vectors." *Journal of Economic Dynamics and Control* (1988), 231-254.

Johansen, Soren and Juselius, Katerina. "Some Structural Hypotheses in a Multivariate Cointegration Analysis of the Purchasing Power Parity and the Uncovered Interest Parity for the U.K." *Journal of Econometrics* 53 (1992), 211-244.

King, Robert G. and Watson, Mark W. "Testing Long-Run Neutrality." Federal Reserve Bank of Richmond *Economic Quarterly* (83) 3 (1997), 69-101.

Koustas, Zisimos and Serletis, Apostolos. "On the Fisher Effect." *Journal of Monetary Economics* (1998).

Kugler, P. and Lenz, Carlos. "Multivariate Cointegration Analysis and the Long-Run Validity of PPP." *The Review of Economics and Statistics* (1993), 180-184.

Kydland, Finn E. and Prescott Edward C. "Time to build and Aggregate Fluctuations." Econometrica 50 (6), (1982), 1345-1370.

Lothian, James R. and Taylor, Mark P. "Real Exchange Rate Behavior: The Recent Float from the Perspective of the Past Two Centuries." *Journal of Political Economy* 104 (1996), 488-509

Lucas, Robert E. "Econometric Testing of the Natural Rate Hypothesis." In Otto Eckstein, ed., The Econometrics of Price Determination, Washington: Board of Governors of the Federal Reserve System, 1972.

McCallum, Bennett T. "On Low-Frequency Estimates of Long-Run Relationships in Macroeconomics." *Journal of Monetary Economics* 14 (1984), 3-14.

Nelson, Charles R. and Plosser, Charles I. "Trends and Random Walks in Macroeconomic Time Series: Some Evidence and Implications." *Journal of Monetary Economics* 10 (1982), 139-162.

Nelson, Daniel B. (1991), "Conditional Heteroskedasticity in Asset Returns: A New Approach", *Econometrica*, 59, p. 347-370.

Newey, Whitney K.., and West, Kenneth D. (1987), "A Simple, Positive Semi-definite, Heteroskedasticity and Autocorrelation Consistent Covariance Matrix", *Econometrica*, 55, p. 703-708.

Newey, Whitney K. and West, Kenneth D. "A Simple, Positive Semi-definite, Heteroscedasticity and Autocorrelation Consistent Covariance Matrix." *Econometrica* 55 (1987), 703-708.

Patel, Jayendu. "Purchasing Power Parity as a Long-Run Relation." *Journal of Applied Econometrics* 5 (1990), 367-379.

Perron, Pierre. "Trends and Random Walks in Macroeconomic Time Series." *Journal of Economic Dynamics and Control* 12 (1988), 297-332.

Perron, Pierre and Vogelsang, Timothy J. "Nonstationarity and Level Shifts with an Application to Purchasing Power Parity." *Journal of Business and Economic Statistics* 10 (1992), 301-320.

Phillips, P.C.B. "Time Series Regression With a Unit Root." *Econometrica* 55 (1987), 277-301.

Phylaktis, Kate and Kassimatis, Yiannis. "Does the Real Exchange Rate Follow a Random Walk: The Pacific Basin Perspective." *Journal of International Money and Finance* 13 (1994), 476-495.

Pippenger, Michael K. "Cointegration Tests of Purchasing Power Parity: The Case of Swiss Exchange Rates." *Journal of International Money and Finance* 12 (1993), 46-61.

Said, S.E., and Dickey, D.A. "Testing for Unit Roots in Autoregressive-Moving Average Models of Unknown Order", Biometrica, 71 (1984), 599-607.

Sargent, Thomas J. "A Note on the Accelerationist Controversy." *Journal of Money Credit and Banking* 3 (1988), 111-156.

Serletis, Apostolos. (1994), "Common Stochastic Trends in a System of East European Black-Market Exchange Rates", *Applied Financial Economics*, 4, 23-31.

Serletis, Apostolos. "Maximum Likelihood Cointegration Tests of Purchasing Power Parity: Evidence from 17 OECD Countries." *Weltwirtschaftliches Archiv* 130 (1994), 476-493.

Serletis, Apostolos., and Gogas, Periklis. (1997), "Chaos in East European Black Market Exchange Rates"" *Research in Economics*, 51, p. 359-385.

Serletis, Apostolos and Koustas, Zisimos. "The Phillips Curve." *Journal of Money Credit and Banking*, forthcoming (1998)

Serletis, Apostolos and Krause, David. "Empirical Evidence on the Long-Run Neutrality Hypothesis Using Low-Frequency International Data." Economics Letters, 50 (1996), 323-327.

Serletis, Apostolos and Zimonopoulos, Gregory. "Breaking Trend Functions in Real Exchange Rates: Evidence from 17 OECD Countries." *Journal of Macroeconomics*, forthcoming (1997).

Taylor, Mark P. and McMahon, Patrick C. "Long-Run Prchasing Power Parity in the 1920s." European Economic Review, 32 (1988), 179-197.

Theil, H. (1961), *Economic Forecasts and Policy*, Amsterdam: North-Holland, p. 30-37.